SMITH
WIGGLESWORTH ON THE
ANOINTING

WHITAKER
HOUSE

Whitaker House gratefully acknowledges and thanks Glenn Gohr and the entire staff of the Flower Pentecostal Heritage Center in Springfield, Missouri, and Rev. Desmond Cartwright of the Donald Gee Centre for Pentecostal and Charismatic Research in Mattersey, England, for graciously assisting us in compiling the sermons of Smith Wigglesworth for publication in this book.

Unless otherwise noted, Scripture quotations are taken from the *New King James Version* (NKJV), © 1979, 1980, 1982 by Thomas Nelson, Inc. Used by permission. All rights reserved.

Scripture quotations marked (KJV) are taken from the *King James Version* of the Bible.

Scripture quotations marked (MOFFAT) are from The Bible: The James Moffatt Translation, ©1922, 1924, 1925, 1926, 1935, by Harper & Row, Publishers, Inc. ©1950, 1952, 1953, 1954, by James A. R. Moffatt.

WIGGLESWORTH ON THE ANOINTING

ISBN: 978-0-88368-530-3
eBook ISBN: 978-1-60374-344-0
Printed in the United States of America
© 2000 by Whitaker House

Whitaker House
1030 Hunt Valley Circle
New Kensington, PA 15068

Library of Congress Cataloging-in-Publication Data
Wigglesworth, Smith, 1859–1947.
    Wigglesworth on the anointing.
        p.   cm.
    ISBN 0-88368-530-2 (trade paper) 1.
    Anointing of the Holy Spirit. I. Title.
BT123.W47 1999
234'.13—dc21   99-049228

This book has been printed digitally and produced in a standard specification in order to ensure its continuing availability.

CONTENTS

INTRODUCTION

An encounter with Smith Wigglesworth was an unforgettable experience. This seems to be the universal reaction of all who knew him or heard him speak. Smith Wigglesworth was a simple yet remarkable man who was used in an extraordinary way by our extraordinary God. He had a contagious and inspiring faith. Under his ministry, thousands of people came to salvation, committed themselves to a deeper faith in Christ, received the baptism in the Holy Spirit, and were miraculously healed. The power that brought these kinds of results was the presence of the Holy Spirit, who filled Smith Wigglesworth and used him in bringing the good news of the Gospel to people all over the world. Wigglesworth gave glory to God for everything that was accomplished through his ministry, and he wanted people to understand his work only in this context, because his sole desire was that people would see Jesus and not himself.

Smith Wigglesworth was born in England in 1859. Immediately after his conversion as a boy, he had a concern for the salvation of others and won people to Christ, including his mother. Even so, as a young man, he could not express himself well enough to give a testimony in church, much less preach a sermon. Wigglesworth said that his mother had the same difficulty in expressing herself that he did. This family trait, coupled with the fact that he had no formal education because he began working twelve hours a day at the age of seven to help support the family, contributed to Wigglesworth's awkward speaking style. He became a plumber by trade, yet he continued to devote himself to winning many people to Christ on an individual basis.

In 1882, he married Polly Featherstone, a vivacious young woman who loved God and had a gift of preaching and evangelism. It was she who taught him to read and who became his closest confidant and strongest supporter. They both had compassion for the poor and needy in their community, and they opened a mission, at which Polly preached. Significantly, people were miraculously healed when Wigglesworth prayed for them.

In 1907, Wigglesworth's circumstances changed dramatically when, at the age of forty-eight, he was baptized in the Holy Spirit. Suddenly, he had a new power that enabled him to preach, and even his wife was amazed at the transformation. This was the beginning of what became a worldwide evangelistic and healing ministry that reached thousands. He eventually ministered in the United States, Australia, South Africa, and all over Europe. His ministry extended up to the time of his death in 1947.

Several emphases in Smith Wigglesworth's life and ministry characterize him: a genuine, deep compassion for the unsaved and sick; an unflinching belief in the Word of God; a desire that Christ should increase and he should decrease (John 3:30); a belief that he was called to exhort people to enlarge their faith and trust in God;

an emphasis on the baptism in the Holy Spirit with the manifestation of the gifts of the Spirit as in the early church; and a belief in complete healing for everyone of all sickness.

Smith Wigglesworth was called "The Apostle of Faith" because absolute trust in God was a constant theme of both his life and his messages. In his meetings, he would quote passages from the Word of God and lead lively singing to help build people's faith and encourage them to act on it. He emphasized belief in the fact that God could do the impossible. He had great faith in what God could do, and God did great things through him.

Wigglesworth's unorthodox methods were often questioned. As a person, Wigglesworth was reportedly courteous, kind, and gentle. However, he became forceful when dealing with the Devil, whom he believed caused all sickness. Wigglesworth said the reason he spoke bluntly and acted forcefully with people was that he knew he needed to get their attention so they could focus on God. He also had such anger toward the Devil and sickness that he acted in a seemingly rough way. When he prayed for people to be healed, he would often hit or punch them at the place of their problem or illness. Yet, no one was hurt by this startling treatment. Instead, they were remarkably healed. When he was asked why he treated people in this manner, he said that he was not hitting the people but that he was hitting the Devil. He believed that Satan should never be treated gently or allowed to get away with anything. About twenty people were reportedly raised from the dead after he prayed for them. Wigglesworth himself was healed of appendicitis and kidney stones, after which his personality softened and he was more gentle with those who came to him for prayer for healing. His abrupt manner in ministering may be attributed to the fact that he was very serious about his calling and got down to business quickly.

Although Wigglesworth believed in complete healing, he encountered illnesses and deaths that were difficult to understand. These included the deaths of his wife and son, his daughter's lifelong deafness, and his own battles with kidney stones and sciatica.

He often seemed paradoxical: compassionate but forceful, blunt but gentle, a well-dressed gentleman whose speech was often ungrammatical or confusing. However, he loved God with everything he had, he was steadfastly committed to God and to His Word, and he didn't rest until he saw God move in the lives of those who needed Him.

In 1936, Smith Wigglesworth prophesied about what we now know as the charismatic movement. He accurately predicted that the established mainline denominations would experience revival and the gifts of the Spirit in a way that would surpass even the Pentecostal movement. Wigglesworth did not live to see the renewal, but as an evangelist and prophet with a remarkable healing ministry, he had a tremendous influence on both the Pentecostal and charismatic movements, and his example and influence on believers is felt to this day.

Without the power of God that was so obviously present in his life and ministry, we might not be reading transcripts of his sermons, for his spoken messages were often disjointed and ungrammatical. However, true gems of spiritual insight shine through them because of the revelation he received through the Holy Spirit. It was his life of complete devotion and belief in God and his reliance on the Holy Spirit that brought the life-changing power of God into his messages.

As you read this book, it is important to remember that Wigglesworth's works span a period of several decades, from the early 1900s to the 1940s. They were originally presented as spoken rather than written messages, and necessarily retain some of the flavor of a church service or prayer meeting. Some of the messages were Bible studies that Wigglesworth led at various conferences. At his meetings, he would often speak in tongues and give the interpretation, and these messages have been included as well. Because of Wigglesworth's unique style, the sermons and Bible studies in this book have been edited for clarity, and archaic expressions that would be unfamiliar to modern readers have been updated.

In conclusion, we hope that as you read these words of Smith Wigglesworth, you will truly sense his complete trust and unwavering faith in God and take to heart one of his favorite sayings: "Only believe!"

1

ABIDING IN POWER

Abide in the presence of the power of God, where victory is assured. If we remain in the right place with God, He can do anything with our lives. He can work through us. There was a power and majesty that fell on Jesus when He received the Spirit (Matt. 3:16–17). He was no longer the same. He had received the mighty anointing power of God. He attained submission, and as He submitted, He was more and more covered with the power and led by the Spirit. He came out of the wilderness more full of God, more clothed with the Spirit, and more ready for the fight. (See Matthew 4.) The empowerment had such an effect on Him that other people saw it and flocked to hear Him, and great blessing came to the land.

The Holy Spirit coming upon an individual changes him and fertilizes his spiritual life. What things are possible if we reach this place and remain in it, that is, abide in it! Only one thing is going to accomplish the purpose of God, which is to be filled with the Spirit. We must yield and submit until our bodies are saturated with God, so that, at any moment, God's will can be revealed. We need a great hunger and thirst for God. Thousands must be brought to a knowledge of the truth. This will only be brought about by human instrumentality, when the instrument is at a place where he will say all that the Holy Spirit directs him to. *"Be still, and know that I am God"* (Ps. 46:10). This place is the place of tranquillity, where we know that He is controlling us and that He moves us by the mighty power of His Spirit.

Ezekiel said, *"I prophesied as I was commanded"* (Ezek. 37:7). He did what he was told to do. It takes more to live in that place than in any other that I know of—to live in the place where you hear God's voice. Only by the power of the Spirit can you quickly do as you are told.

We must stay in the place where we see God, where we always hear His voice, and from where He sends us with messages that bring life and power and victory.

2

"YOU SHALL RECEIVE POWER"

Y*ou shall receive power when the Holy Spirit has come upon you"* (Acts 1:8). The context of this passage is that the disciples had been asking whether the Lord would at that time restore the kingdom to Israel (v. 6). Christ told them that it was not for them to know the times and seasons that the Father had put in His own power, but He promised them that when they received the Holy Spirit, they would receive power to witness for Him in all the world (vv. 7–8). To receive the Holy Spirit is to receive power with God and power with men.

There is a power that is of God, and there is a power that is of Satan. When the Holy Spirit fell in the early days of the Pentecostal outpouring we are experiencing, a number of Spiritists came to our meetings. They thought we had received something like they had, and they were coming to have a good time. They filled the two front rows of our mission. When the power of God fell, these imitators began their shaking and muttering under the power of the Devil. The Spirit of the Lord came mightily on me, and I cried out, "Now, you devils, clear out of here!" And out they went. I followed them right out into the street, and then they turned around and cursed me. There was power from below, but it was no match for the power of the Holy Spirit, and they soon had to retreat.

POWER FROM ON HIGH

The Lord wants all saved people to receive *"power from on high"* (Luke 24:49)—power to witness, power to act, power to live, and power to show forth the divine manifestations of God within. The power of God will take you out of your own plans and put you into the plan of God. You will be unclothed and divested of what is purely of yourself and put into a divine order. The Lord will change you and put His mind where yours was, and thus enable you to have *"the mind of Christ"* (1 Cor. 2:16). Instead of your working according to your own plan, it will be God working in you and through you to do His own good pleasure through the power of the Spirit within (Phil. 2:13).

Someone has said that you are no good until you have your "I" knocked out. Christ must reign within, and life in the Holy Spirit means, at all times, the subjection of your own will to make way for the working out of the *"good and acceptable and perfect will of God"* within (Rom. 12:2).

The Lord Jesus commanded that the disciples should tarry until they were *"endued with power from on high"* (Luke 24:49). In Acts 2, we read how the Spirit of God came. He comes in the same way today, and we don't know of the Holy Spirit coming in any other way.

Once, I was holding a meeting in London, and at the close of the meeting, a man came to me and said, "We are not allowed to hold meetings in this hall after eleven o'clock, and we would like you to come home with us. I am so hungry for God." His wife said that she, too, was hungry for God, and so I agreed to go with them. At about twelve-thirty, we arrived at their house. The man began stirring up the fire and said, "Now we will have a good supper." I said to them, "I did not come here for your warm fire, your supper, or your bed. I came here because I thought you were hungry to get more of God." We got down to pray, and at about three-thirty, the Lord baptized the wife, and she spoke in tongues as the Spirit gave utterance (Acts 2:4). At about five o'clock, I spoke to the husband and asked how he was getting on. He replied, "God has broken my iron, stubborn will." He had not received the baptism, but God had worked a mighty work within him.

The following day, at his business, everyone could tell that a great change had come to him. Before, he had been a walking terror. The men who worked for him had looked upon him as a regular devil because of the way he had acted, but coming into contact with the power of God that night had completely changed him. Before this, he had made a religious profession, but he had never truly entered into the experience of the new birth until that night when the power of God surged so mightily through his home. A short while afterward, I went to this man's home, and his two sons ran to me and kissed me, saying, "We have a new father." Prior to this, these boys had often said to their mother, "Mother, we cannot stand it in the home any longer. We will have to leave." But the Lord changed the whole situation that night as we prayed together. On my second visit, the Lord baptized this man in the Holy Spirit. The Holy Spirit will reveal false positions, pull the mask off any *"refuge of lies"* (Isa. 28:17), and clean up and remove all false conditions. When the Holy Spirit came in, that man's house and business, and he himself, were entirely changed.

THE HOLY SPIRIT COMES TO EMPOWER

When the Holy Spirit comes, He comes to empower you to be an effective witness. At one time, we were holding some special meetings, and I was out distributing handbills. I went into a shoe-maker's store, and there was a man with a green shade and a cloth over his eyes. My heart looked up to the Lord, and I had the witness within that He was ready to change any condition. The man was crying, "Oh! Oh! *Oh!*" I asked, "What's the trouble?" He told me he was suffering from great inflammation and burning. I said, "I rebuke this condition in Jesus' name." Instantly, the Lord healed him. He took off the shade and the cloth, and said, "Look, it is all gone." I believe the Lord wants us to enter into real activity and dare to do for Him. "*You shall receive power when the Holy Spirit has come upon you*" (Acts 1:8).

At one time, a lady wrote and asked if I could go and help her. She said that she was blind, having two blood clots behind her eyes. When I reached the house, they brought the blind woman to me. We were together for some time, and then the power of God fell. Rushing to the window, she exclaimed, "I can see! Oh, I can see! The blood is gone; I can see." She then inquired about receiving the Holy Spirit and confessed that, for ten years, she had been fighting our position. She said, "I could not bear these tongues, but God has settled the whole thing today. I now want the baptism in the Holy Spirit." The Lord graciously baptized her in the Spirit.

THE HOLY SPIRIT WILL COME WHEN A PERSON IS CLEANSED

The Holy Spirit will come when a person is cleansed. There must be a purging of the old life. I never saw anyone baptized who was not clean within. I never saw a man baptized who smoked. We take it for granted that anyone who is seeking the fullness of the

Spirit is free from such things as these. You cannot expect the third person of the Trinity to come into an unclean temple. There first must be a confession of all that is wrong, and a cleansing in the precious blood of Jesus Christ.

I remember being in a meeting where there was a man seeking the baptism, and he looked like he was in trouble. He was very restless, and finally he said to me, "I will have to go." I said, "What's up?" He said, "God is unveiling things to me, and I feel so unworthy." I said, "Repent of everything that is wrong." He continued to tarry, and the Lord continued to search his heart. These times of waiting on God for the fullness of the Spirit are times when He searches the heart and tests the mind (Jer. 17:10). Later, the man said to me, "I have a hard thing to do, the hardest thing I have ever had to do." I said to him, "Tell the Lord you will do it, and never mind the consequences." He agreed, and the next morning, he had to take a thirty-mile ride and go with a bag of gold to a certain party with whom he dealt. This man who was seeking the baptism had a hundred head of cattle, and he bought all his feed at a certain place. He always paid his accounts on a certain day, but one day he missed. He was always so punctual in paying his accounts that when the people of this firm later went over their books, they thought they must have made a mistake in not crediting the man with the money, and so they sent him a receipt. The man never intended not to pay the account, but if you delay doing a right thing, the Devil will see to it that you never do it. But when the man was seeking the Lord that night, the Lord dealt with him on this point, and he had to go and straighten the thing out the next morning. He paid the account, and then the Lord baptized him in the Spirit. Those who carry the vessels of the Lord must be clean, must be holy (Isa. 52:11).

THE HOLY SPIRIT BRINGS A RICH REVELATION OF CHRIST

When the Holy Spirit comes, He always brings a rich revelation of Christ. Christ becomes so real to you that when, under the power of the Spirit, you begin to express your love and praise to Him, you find yourself speaking in another tongue. Oh, it is a wonderful thing! At one time, I belonged to a group who believed that they had received the baptism in the Spirit without the speaking in tongues. There are many people like that today; however, if you can go with them to a prayer meeting, you will find them asking the Lord again and again to baptize them in the Spirit. Why all this asking if they really have received the baptism? I have never heard people who have received the baptism in the Holy Spirit in accordance with the original pattern asking the Lord to give them the Holy Spirit. They know for certain that He has come.

I was once traveling from Belgium to England. When I landed in England, I received a request to stop at a place between Harwich and Colchester. The people there were delighted that God had sent me, and they told me of a special case they wanted me to pray for. They said, "We have a brother here who believes in the Lord, and he is paralyzed from his hips downward. He cannot stand on his legs, and he has been in this condition for twenty years." They took me to this man, and as I saw him there in his chair, I put the question to him, "What is the greatest desire in your heart?" He said, "Oh, if I could only receive the Holy Spirit!" I was somewhat surprised at this answer, and I laid my hands on his head and said, *"Receive the Holy Spirit"* (John 20:22). Instantly, the power of God fell on him, and he began breathing very heavily. He rolled off the chair, and there he lay like a bag of potatoes, utterly helpless. I like anything that God does. I like to watch God working. There he was, with his great, fat body, and his head was moving just as though it was on a swivel. Then, to our joy, he began speaking in tongues. I had my eyes on every bit of him, and as I saw the condition of his legs, I said, "Those legs can never carry that body." Then I looked up and said, "Lord, tell me what to do." The Holy Spirit carries out the will of Jesus Christ and the Father. If you want to know the mind of God, you must have the Holy Spirit to bring God's latest thought to you and to tell you what to do. The Lord said to me, "Command him in My name to walk." But I missed it, of course. I said to the people there, "Let's see if we can lift him up." But we could not lift him. It was as if he weighed a ton. I cried, "Oh, Lord, forgive me." I repented of doing the wrong thing, and then the Lord said to me again, "Command him to walk." I said to him, "Arise in the name of Jesus." His legs were immediately strengthened. Did he walk? He ran all around. A month after this, he walked ten miles and back. He has a Pentecostal ministry now. When the power of the Holy Spirit is present, things will happen.

There is still more for us all, praise the Lord. This is only the beginning. So far, we have only touched the fringe of things. There is so much more for us if we will only yield to God.

Do you want to receive the Spirit? *"If you then, being evil, know how to give good gifts to your children, how much more will your heavenly Father give the Holy Spirit to those who ask Him!"* (Luke 11:13). I am a father, and I want to give my boys the very best. We human fathers are only finite, but our heavenly Father is infinite. There is no limit to the power and blessing He has stored up for those who love Him. *"Be filled with the Spirit"* (Eph. 5:18).

3

THIRSTING FOR FULLNESS

In John 7:37–39, our Lord was in a present- tense position. He was in the activity and the actual workings of the power of God, and He knew that He was empowered or driven or led by a power that has to be the world's share. Believers have to reach this blessed attitude and be clothed within with the rays of heaven's light so that they may be exactly as He was—with a clear idea of the knowledge of satanic forces, of the powers of God, of the limitations of Satan, and the powerfulness of the Almighty. Let us read from John:

> On the last day, that great day of the feast, Jesus stood and cried out, saying, "If anyone thirsts, let him come to Me and drink. He who believes in Me, as the Scripture has said, out of his heart will flow rivers of living water." But this He spoke concerning the Spirit, whom those believing in Him would receive; for the Holy Spirit was not yet given, because Jesus was not yet glorified.
>
> (John 7:37–39)

Here, Jesus was speaking of what may be the position of every believer, now that the Holy Spirit has been given. At that time, He was speaking of it in the future tense; He knew that everybody who received what He was waiting to give would be the people who were ready for the power when it came.

THIRSTING FOR GOD

The background to this Scripture passage is that the crowds had been to Jerusalem to worship and were returning dry and barren and needing blessing. Beloved, I believe that God has a great plan in this for us to see. Those who were thirsty could have something that morning. Those who were hungry could have something that morning. They had been to Jerusalem making their offerings; they were going away dry and helpless, and He was the only One who could cry out this message: *"If anyone thirsts, let him come to Me and drink....[for] out of his heart will flow rivers of living water"* (John 7:37–38). Jesus spoke this of the Spirit, who would be given after He was glorified (v. 39).

Now, keep in mind the following facts. First, you must know that there is a dry condition existing everywhere today. I find it all over. People are longing for a fullness. There never was such a cry, and beloved, it is because the Scriptures are being fulfilled. The *"early [former]...rain"* (James 5:7) fell in a very blessed way, clothing the apostles with power (Luke 24:49), and the acts of the apostles came forth because they dared to act. We see the deliverance of the captives, the mightiness flowing through like a river until thousands and tens of thousands were saved by the power of the former rain, which was by the Spirit. But in these last days, God will pour out upon all flesh the *"latter rain"* (James 5:7), and I believe all flesh will feel the effects of it. It will not be possible for anyone to miss it. They may refuse it, but it will be there for the taking. I believe that God wants us to see that the latter rain has begun to fall. I do not say that we are anywhere near the fullness of it; however, I do see a great thirst for the fullness, and I believe that that thirst is not brought about by visible man. You cannot love righteousness and hate iniquity (Ps. 45:7), nor can you desire purity in any way, through the flesh. Flesh was never subject to the law, nor indeed can it be. The flesh has to come into regeneration, and the regenerated heart is becoming hungry.

God is creating a hunger and thirst. I see it all over. There are people who begin waiting on God, and they do not know what they are waiting for—they have no idea. I believe that God is making the thing so that you cannot get out of it. You may refuse it, and you may come within its reach and come outside the boundaries of it, but it is for you. It is a personal baptism—it is not a church baptism. It is for the body of believers who are to be clothed with the power and unction, or anointing, of the Spirit by this glorious waiting. What do I mean by saying it is not a "church" baptism? Why, I mean that people get their minds on a building when I say "church." You see, it is the believers who compose the "body" —believers in the Lord Jesus Christ—whatever sect or creed or denomination they are. I also tell you that Paul went so far as to say that some people have very strange ideas of who will be ready for the coming of the kingdom. All in Christ will be ready, and you have to decide whether you are in Christ or not. The Scripture says, in the first verse of Romans 8, "*There is therefore now no condemnation to those who are in Christ Jesus, who do not walk according to the flesh, but according to the Spirit.*" If you are there—praise the Lord! That is a good position. I ask the Lord that He will bring us all into that place. What a wonder it will be.

I want you to see that the Master's idea was of a river flowing through everyone who comes to Him. Whatever you think about it,

Jesus wants your salvation to be like a river, and I am sure that Jesus is the ideal for us all.

The lack today is the lack of understanding of that blessed fullness of Christ. He came to do nothing less than to embody us with the same manifestation that He had: the manifestation of "doing." Turning for a moment to Jesus' attitude in the Holy Spirit, I would like you to see a plan there. In Acts 1, we find that Jesus *"began both to do and teach"* (v. 1); the believer should always be so full of the Holy Spirit that he begins to *"do,"* and then he can *"teach."* He must be ready for the man in the street. He must be instantly ready, flowing like a river. He must have three things: ministration, operation, and manifestation, and these three things must always be forthcoming.

We ought to be so full of the manifestation of the power of God that, in the name of Jesus, we can absolutely destroy the power of Satan. We are in the world—not of it (John 17:11, 14). Jesus overcame the world (John 16:33), and we are in the world to subdue it unto God—as overcomers. We are nothing in ourselves, but in Christ *"we are more than conquerors"* (Rom. 8:37) through the blood of Jesus—more than a match for satanic powers in every way. Therefore, may the Lord let us see that we must be loosed from ourselves. For if you examine yourself, you will be natural, but if you look at God, you will be supernatural. If you have a great God, you will have a little Devil; and if you have a big Devil, you will have a little god. May the Lord let us see that we must be so full of the order of the Spirit of life that we are always overcoming *"him who had the power of death, that is, the devil"* (Heb. 2:14).

Jesus was only laying a foundation, which is the new birth unto righteousness. It is the drink at the well; it is receiving Him, and by receiving Him, you may have power to become children of God. For as many as receive Him become the children of God (John 1:12).

So, in the passage we looked at earlier, Jesus was at the temple. The great crowds of people who had thronged the place were dissatisfied as they returned from the Feast of Tabernacles, and Jesus stood and cried, *"If anyone thirsts, let him come to Me and drink'* (John 7:37), and out of that drink will flow *'rivers of living water'* (v. 38)." Now, who does not want these rivers? *"This He spoke concerning the Spirit, whom those believing in Him would receive; for the Holy Spirit was not yet given, because Jesus was not yet glorified"* (v. 39).

Let me, by the grace of God, just put us into the place where we can expect and receive. Now, we know as well as anything that the Day of Pentecost came. We know that Jesus was first received up into glory, and that the angels spoke as He was going away, saying, "This same Jesus will come again." (See Acts 1:4–11.) We know that the disciples tarried at Jerusalem until they were *"endued with power from on high"* (Luke 24:49), and we know that the Holy Spirit came. (See Acts 2:1–4.) Therefore, since we know that the Holy Spirit came, it is wrong for us now to wait for the Holy Spirit.

I know it was personally right, it was divinely right, for those apostles to hear what Jesus said and to tarry for the Holy Spirit; however, it is not right *now* to tarry for the Holy Spirit. Then why do we not all receive the Holy Spirit, you ask? Because our bodies are not ready for it; our temples are not cleansed. When our temples are purified and our minds are put in order so that carnalities and fleshly desires and everything contrary to the Spirit have gone, then the Holy Spirit can take full charge. The Holy Spirit is not a manifestation of carnality. There are any number of people who never read the Word of God who could not be led away by the powers of Satan. But the power of the Holy Spirit is most lovely, divine in all its construction. It is a great refiner. It is full of life, but it is always divine—never natural. If you deal in the flesh after you are baptized in the Holy Spirit, you cease to go on.

Beloved, I want to speak about something greater; something to lift your minds, elevate your thoughts, and bring you into divine ways; something that elevates you out of yourself and into God, out of the world and into a place where you know you have rest for your feet, where you cease from your own works (Heb. 4:10), and where God works in you mightily *"to will and to do for His good pleasure"* (Phil. 2:13).

When I think about a river—a pure, holy, divine river—I say, "What can stand against its inrush?" Wherever it is—in a railway coach, in the street, or in a meeting—its power and flow will always be felt; it will always do its work. Jesus spoke about the Holy Spirit that was to be given. I want you to think about how God gave it, how its coming was manifested, and its reception and its outflow after it had come.

In Acts 2, we find three positions of the Holy Spirit. The first is *"a rushing mighty wind"* (v. 2), and I want you to keep that in mind. The second is *"divided tongues, as of fire"* (v. 3)—keep that also in mind. And the third is the fact of the incoming of the manifestations. Now, keep your mind for a moment on the rushing mighty wind; next, see the divided tongues of fire over every one of the disciples; and then see the incoming and the outflow through it. I am glad that the Holy Spirit is manifested to us as wind, and as fire resting upon a person (v. 3). I am especially glad that the Holy Spirit is a manifestation to us of fire, for fire is wonderful. Then I want you to know that the Holy Spirit is power—these three things.

Can we be filled with a river? How is it possible for a river to flow out of us? A river of water is always an emblem of the Word of God—the Water of Life. Therefore, when the Holy Spirit comes, He clothes and anoints the Christ who is already within the believer, who will be just the same only so much different; the power of the

Spirit of the life of Christ is now being manifested in a new way, for this is the plan of God. You should be filled with the matter of the Word, for that is the life. You will never get to know God better by testimony—testimony should always come through the Word. You will not get to know God better by prayer—prayer has to come out of the Word.

The Word is the only thing that reveals God and is going to be helpful in the world through you. For when the breath and the presence of God come—carrying out the will of God the Father and the Son—the Holy Spirit speaks expressively according to the mind of the Father and the Son. Therefore, when you are filled with the Holy Spirit, then the breath—the power, the unction, the fire—takes hold of the Word of Life, which is Christ, and out of you flow the rivers. God wants to fill us with that divine power so that rivers will flow out of us.

The preparation is the place where Paul had reached when he said he had become *"the least of all"* (Eph. 3:8), where he counted everything as *"dung"* (Phil. 3:8 kjv) compared to the *"excellence of the knowledge of Christ Jesus"* (v. 8), and where he knew that in his flesh there was *"nothing good"* (Rom. 7:18). Then he was in a place of denunciation. If there is anything in you that likes to be seen and heard, it will have to die, for Jesus must have all the glory in a person. It is not possible for you and God to dwell in the same body in fullness. When you come to an end of yourself, that is the beginning of an almightiness of God; however, a little thing may stop the flow.

I have never seen a man keep the anointing of the baptism of the Holy Spirit who drank intoxicating liquors. I have never seen a man manifest and carry forth the order of the baptism of the Holy Spirit who smoked. If these outward things, which can be seen, hinder God from holding sway in our lives, what about the inward things?

It was perfectly right for Jesus to say that a man who looked on *"a woman to lust for her ha[d] already committed adultery...in his heart"* (Matt. 5:28); James said that when you are drawn aside and tempted, it is because of your own lust (James 1:14). Therefore, before the Holy Spirit can have His way within you, you must be cleansed from your own evil appetites; there must be a body prepared for the Holy Spirit. Can it be so? Yes.

INTERPRETATION OF TONGUES

It is the divine plan, which is the inward movement of the Spirit, which is the divine order of Trinity taking hold of nature and transforming it into power and bringing it into a place where out of it flow rivers of living water; light, revelation, open door—intercession, making a way into all darkness, bringing to God the things that are so manifestly declared, that day by day we are the sons of God.

This river flows without an effort. When the Holy Spirit takes hold of you, you will no longer rack your brains or have sleepless nights when preparing your addresses; God will do it. You will have a self-contained library in the Holy Spirit. He has the last thoughts from heaven—the first thoughts for earth. He has everything He wants you to have, and if you have anything that He doesn't want you to have, it is worthless. If you are to be the oracles of God—the apostles of Christ—and as those quickened from the dead, enlarged by the Spirit, intensified with the zeal of the Almighty, and made a river, you will have to be on fire, for nothing but fire will make the water boil. Oh, it is lovely.

You see, beloved, the grace of God is so full that He makes you know that you have ceased to be. If I could only plant that into your heart. Is it possible? Yes, this is the great plan of God for you. It is the sole purpose of God, a greater purpose than you can conceive of, and it is God's thought for you. He has no less a plan for you than to make you a son of God with power according to the Resurrection. I tell you that the incarnation of God by the Spirit is for the purpose of unveiling the glory; let in a cloudburst and let it make inroads into you until there are new rivers. Oh, for your old rivers to be dried up and the new river by the cloudburst of heaven to make a new plan for you for all time, for He is able to do these things in the Spirit!

God is able to do this for any one of us who will yield to Him. In the Bible, you will find that there are Abraham, Isaac, and Jacob. Abraham was the father of all; Isaac was the seed of all; and Jacob was the failure of all. However, you never find God mentioning Abraham and Isaac without bringing in Jacob. Can Jacobs be changed? (There are plenty of them.) Yes. That is the plan of God— to make the Jacobs into Israels.

God took the waywardness and the supplanting of Jacob and changed him so that he no longer followed those ways. When his sons were going into Egypt to see Joseph after they had brought all the money back, he told them to take double and to take a present and to take this and that. (See Genesis 42:29–43:15.) What a difference! When he was with Laban, he took the lot (see Genesis 30:25–43); but God had changed him. Oh, beloved, I tell you that when we get to see that God Almighty would always bring in the weaknesses with His power, when we see that He has a plan for us, when we know that God can take our weaknesses and make them power, when we know that He can take our weaknesses and depravity and make us holy, then we know we have a God of immensity. He takes the first, establishes the second, and the first is not mentioned again. "*The first man was of the earth, made of dust; the second Man is the Lord from heaven*" (1 Cor. 15:47). God wants us to know that the power of the Christ of God is for the purpose of making the first man heavenly. Oh, hallelujah!

INTERPRETATION OF TONGUES

It is He who created all things for Himself who has come in to create us for Himself, that we may be no longer of the outward but inward perfection with Him who has created us in power and might and revelation—gods in the earth. Hallelujah—clothed with power!

Beloved, listen to this: "*Philip said to Him, 'Lord, show us the Father'*" (John 14:8). Note Jesus' answer: "*He who has seen Me has seen the Father*" (v. 9). Oh, beloved, the time had to come that when they looked at Philip, they had to see Jesus. The world does not have to see us; it has to see Jesus. It can only be convinced in this way that Jesus has been formed in the hearts and lives of His people. Then again, the same Word must come to us in power. Take note of what it says: "*The words that I speak to you I do not speak on My own authority; but the Father who dwells in Me does the works*" (John 14:10).

When that reality comes to our lost state, what a transformation! When the Holy Spirit comes, He does the work. You are only the instrument; you are the vessel. But, glory to God, He condescended to dwell in us; praise the Lamb! "*The words that I speak to you I do not speak on My own authority; but the Father who dwells in Me does the works.*" How lovely to be filled with such an incarnation of God's order that the power of the Spirit of the life of Jesus flows through you, and you are a new creation of the Spirit under the mighty power of God. *"He who has seen Me has seen the Father"* (v. 9).

Directly after the baptism of the Holy Spirit came, those crooked, indifferent, and peculiar disciples were transformed until one day Peter and John came down and mingled with the people, who said, "They are unlearned and ignorant, but we see that they have been with Jesus." (See Acts 4:13.) Can people say that about us? Have we been with Jesus? Do not think that you will comfort people by singing wonderful hymns—even though they are lovely. Do not think that you will comfort people in any other way but by the Word of God being manifested in you, revealing that you have been with Jesus. There must be *"the law of the Spirit of life in Christ Jesus"* (Rom. 8:2) that will put to death every other thing.

It is one thing to read the Word of God; it is another thing to believe it. It is possible to be real, earnest, zealous, and to fast, and yet not to have faith. And do you not know that one little bit of faith that can only come through the Word of God is worth more than all your crying, all your rolling on the floor, all your screaming, and everything? Beloved, God is better than anything.

May the Holy Spirit give us today an inward knowledge of what it is to believe. It is God's purpose to make every believer subdue everything and to make you *"perfect and complete"* (James 1:4) and victorious.

4

PENTECOSTAL MANIFESTATIONS

The birth of the church was announced by a *"rushing mighty wind"* (Acts 2:2), a tornado from heaven. Moffatt translates Acts 2:1–2, *"During the course of the day of Pentecost they were all together, when suddenly there came a sound from heaven like a violent blast of wind"* (MOFFATT). And all of the assembled company came under the power of what was symbolized as a mighty tornado, *"a violent blast."* Their whole beings were moved by it, so that onlookers thought they were full of new wine. The unnatural movement of their bodies was followed by a supernatural movement of their tongues, for they spoke in other tongues *"as the Spirit gave them utterance"* (v. 4). Thus they received the enduement of *"power from on high"* (Luke 24:49).

The crowd that was in Jerusalem for Pentecost saw the movements and heard the sounds. The sounds were comprehensible—some of them. The movements were incomprehensible—most of them. Some were amazed—those who could comprehend the languages—and the others were confounded. The latter could not understand the languages, but they thought they could understand the motions, and they interpreted them as the actions of drunken people. Therefore, some were amazed, others mocked—but none understood at first what was really happening.

The motto of a cold, indifferent, worldly church is "Respectability and decorum"—respectability inspired by one who is far from respectable, that is, Satan. A generation that prides itself on its outer respectability and decorum despises the manifestations of the Spirit of God. Nevertheless, it is written, *"The manifestation of the Spirit is given to each one for the profit of all"* (1 Cor. 12:7).

David danced or leaped before the ark of the Lord; he was considered vile, or undignified, by his wife Michal, the daughter of the former king. The daughter of Saul accused the anointed of God of vileness in manifestation, lack of respectability, lack of decorum before the ark of the Lord.

Did David stop when his own wife derided him? Did he acquiesce to the formalism she represented? He declared, *"I will be even more undignified than this"* (2 Sam. 6:22). It was as if he had said, "If occasion requires it, I will leap higher and dance more."

There is great danger when some churches who have known the manifestation of the Spirit in days gone by desire to become so respectable and decorous that the supernatural is ruled out of their meetings. We need people like Peter today who can say, in explanation of the Pentecostal phenomenon in our midst, *"These are not drunk, as you suppose....This is what was spoken by the prophet Joel"* (Acts 2:15–16). If we become so ultra-respectable and decorous that we rule out the supernatural, Peter will have nothing to apologize for. He will have to say, *"'This was what was spoken by the prophet Joel,'* but it is gone now." If that happens, we may as well write this upon our assemblies: *"Ichabod"*—*"the glory has departed"* (1 Sam. 4:21). If we cease to be undignified, Michal will welcome us home.

There must be no compromise with Michals, with those who hate the supernatural, or they will draw us from the presence of the ark and cause us to cease to be joyful in the presence of the Lord. Michal would have been quite content to have the ark stay where it was. (See 2 Samuel 6:12–16.)

Pentecost came with the sound of a mighty rushing wind, a violent blast from heaven! Heaven has not exhausted its blasts, but our danger is that we are getting frightened of them. The apostles were not. They experienced a repetition of God's Pentecostal power. After they were threatened not to speak any longer in the name of Jesus, they lifted up their voices to God in one accord, and prayed,

> *Lord, look on their threats, and grant to Your servants that with all boldness they may speak Your word, by stretching out Your hand to heal, and that signs and wonders may be done through the name of Your holy Servant Jesus.* (Acts 4:29–30)

The place was shaken where they were assembled together, and all were filled afresh with the Holy Spirit. Pentecost repeated! Manifestation again! All were filled—their mouths and all! *"And they spoke the word of God with"*—what? Hesitation, moderation, timidity? No, they were even more undignified. *"They spoke the word of God with boldness"* (v. 31, emphasis added). And the signs and wonders increased. They never resented the first manifestations on their bodies on the Day of Pentecost, and they prayed and received the second experience. Even the place was shaken this time.

Our God is an active God. His thunder is just as loud today as it was in the first century. His lightning is just as vivid as it was in the days of the early church. The sound of the mighty rushing wind is just the same today as it was on the Day of Pentecost. Pray for the violent blasts of wind from heaven, expect them, and you will get them. And do not be afraid of them.

Let God deal with the Michals. David did not compromise. He was willing to have even more manifestations of the Spirit. "*I will be even more undignified than this*" (2 Sam. 6:22). We can have Pentecost plus Pentecost, if we wish. God's arm is not shortened, nor is His ear heavy (Isa. 59:1). He wants to show His hand and the strength of His arm today in convincing a denying world by sight, sound, and instruction. Take note of Conybeare's translation of 1 Thessalonians 5:19: "Quench not the manifestation of the Spirit."

5

NOT DRUNK BUT FILLED

And do not be drunk with wine, in which is dissipation; but be filled with the Spirit, speaking to one another in psalms and hymns and spiritual songs, singing and making melody in your heart to the Lord, giving thanks always for all things to God the Father in the name of our Lord Jesus Christ.
—Ephesians 5:18–20

We must see to it that we are filled with the Holy Spirit's power and be careful not to rest in any gift. We have here the contrary spectacle of a man drunk with wine. What are the special characteristics of a man so possessed? He is not cautious; he is under the control of another spirit that manages him and is believed by him. We must be careful not to choose, but to let God's Holy Spirit manage our lives. We must not smooth down and explain away, but rather *"stir up the gift"* (2 Tim. 1:6); we must allow God's Spirit to disturb us and disturb us and disturb us until we yield and yield and yield and the possibility in God's mind for us becomes an established fact in our lives, with the rivers in evidence meeting the needs of a dying world.

The drunken man is not concerned with what people think or who sees him or what language he utters—he is under the control of another. So let us be careful not to take control. God's Spirit, which is upon us, filling us, is better than our best, and will press us on to a zeal for God as was manifested in our Lord. When Jesus threw the moneychangers out of the temple, His disciples remembered that it was written, *"Zeal for Your house has eaten Me up"* (John 2:17).

Oh, to be pressed on in this way, unreserved, for God! To use our mouths, our brains, our all for Him! To be filled with the Holy Spirit. Is it for us? Oh, yes! *"The promise is to you and to your children, and to all who are afar off, as many as the Lord our God will call"* (Acts 2:39). One passion must possess us—to be filled with the Holy Spirit. Are we so thoughtful (that is, do we have God's thoughts alone and not ours) so that God may have us all to Himself? *"Speaking to one another in psalms and hymns and spiritual songs, singing and making melody in your heart to the Lord"* (Eph. 5:19). A drunken man has his thoughts, his mouth, his body, under the control of another. So our thoughts, our mouths, our bodies, must be under the control of God's Holy Spirit. Is it not lovely? Spiritual songs are the language of the learned. We cannot rest until we are quite full.

What has the Holy Spirit come to do? To convict the world of sin. *"When He has come, He will convict the world of sin"* (John 16:8). Now! Through His indwelling pressure in the hearts of His children. *"Do you not know that your body is the temple of the Holy Spirit?…Therefore glorify God in your body"* (1 Cor. 6:19–20). We cannot convict the world of sin unless we remain in the place where He can rest in His love and joy over us with singing (Zeph. 3:17).

"He brought me to the banqueting house, and his banner over me was love" (Songs 2:4).

"Giving thanks always for all things to God the Father in the name of our Lord Jesus Christ" (Eph. 5:20). If we are filled with the Spirit, then, in the hard place where the test comes, like the three Hebrew children, Shadrach, Meshach, and Abednego, our testimony is, *"We have no need to answer you in this matter....Our God whom we serve is able to deliver us from the burning fiery furnace, and He will deliver us"* (Dan. 3:16–17). You cannot give thanks under such circumstances unless you are filled with the Spirit. *"You are not your own"* (1 Cor. 6:19). You mothers have experienced situations in which your child has said, "Mother! Mother! Mother! My brother has broken the sink upstairs!" The whole house is in a tumult! You can quiet them in the Spirit and still give thanks.

Paul said, *"I know how to be abased, and I know how to abound"* (Phil. 4:12) and *"As having nothing, and yet possessing all things"* (2 Cor. 6:10). He had no need to draw on the bank when he had something; but to have nothing is a rich place; it is a wonderful process! And it only comes to "drunken" people. Suppose a drunken man is singing, muttering, talking. What is it? It is another spirit. So the spiritual man can rest in the Holy Spirit and give thanks. Oh, beloved, to have nothing and yet to possess all things! I can be *"as poor"* (v. 10), and yet, when I feel so, it turns me to the resources of God—to make *"many rich"* (v. 10). What a condition to be in, to grow in!

You know that a drinking man at first takes one glass, then twenty glasses; but when we are seasoned with the grace of God, taking in, taking in until we can rejoice in the hard situation, grace increasing in us from the boundless, endless source, it's wonderful! Only those whom God has in control can give thanks. He abides as a quickening Spirit, an increasing power, when once the Lord has laid hold of us, bringing us to a place of rest in Him.

Let us rejoice, giving thanks all the time—this is the will of God (1 Thess. 5:18). What is God's will toward me? When He gave me Jesus, He gave me all. He laid down a law for me that will always work! Such a law is to continue to believe that Jesus is the Son of God. Can we make ourselves "drunk" in the Lord? We can believe! Simplicity will do it, yieldedness will do it, and faith will assist it. The man who is drunk with wine says that everybody is drunk except him. May God the Holy Spirit make me so unconscious of my condition in the Spirit, so hungry, so thirsty, that I see everyone as having more than me. God can do it; it means much. Jesus says, "I give you My life; it is to become in you a production of what I am." *"Do not be drunk with wine,...but be filled with the Spirit"* (Eph. 5:18).

6

A NEW PLANE OF EXISTENCE

In days gone by, God's people have been persecuted and hunted. In Hebrews 11:38 we read of those *"of whom the world was not worthy. They wandered in deserts and mountains, in dens and caves of the earth."* We live in golden days in comparison—days of sunshine, prosperity, and hopefulness.

If those who have passed on before us wore such beautiful crowns in such times of strain and stress, our mouths should always be pouring forth tidal waves of blessing as the Holy Spirit has His way in these human bodies of ours and produces in us an eternal working: *"For our light affliction, which is but for the moment, is working for us a far more exceeding and eternal weight of glory"* (2 Cor. 4:17).

The baptism of the Holy Spirit is a new plane of existence, a covering with the divine presence, a power burning in our very bones. It is wonderful to be in the place where the truths of the Holy Spirit are so advanced. The day will soon dawn when the Daystar appears

(2 Pet. 1:19 KJV), and our one regret will be our lost opportunities of witnessing for God. May God make us a worthy people who embrace every opportunity.

THE POWER OF THE SPIRIT UPON PAUL

Paul had decided to sail past Ephesus, so that he would not have to spend time in Asia; for he was hurrying to be at Jerusalem, if possible, on the Day of Pentecost. (Acts 20:16)

Paul had seen Jesus by revelation on the road to Damascus, but he wanted to meet with those in Jerusalem who had seen Him as He walked the streets, as He healed the sick and raised the dead. Would you not like to talk with someone who had seen Him? Would you not like to ask, "What was His face like? What was His manner? How did He speak?" *"No man ever spoke like this Man!"* (John 7:46). Lots of people had seen Him around the table and on the roadways, and could testify to His wonderful works. No wonder Paul was hurrying to be at Jerusalem on the Day of Pentecost!

Paul remembered the days of Acts 9 when

as he journeyed he came near Damascus, and suddenly a light shone around him from heaven. So the Lord said to [Ananias], "Arise and go to the street called Straight, and inquire at the house of Judas for one called Saul of Tarsus, for behold, he is praying." And Ananias went his way and entered the house; and laying his hands on him he said, "Brother Saul, the Lord Jesus, who appeared to you on the road as you came, has sent me that you may receive your sight and be filled with the Holy Spirit." Immediately there fell from his eyes something like scales, and

he received his sight at once; and he arose and was baptized.
(Acts 9:3, 11, 17–18)

Paul was stirred as he remembered this mighty baptism in the Spirit, the victory that it had brought him into, and the power to preach the Gospel unlimited and unhindered that effectually worked in him. The mighty unction, or anointing, of the Holy Spirit remained upon him. We see this in the account of what happened at Troas:

When the disciples came together to break bread, Paul, ready to depart the next day, spoke to them and continued his message until midnight. There were many lamps in the upper room where they were gathered together. And in a window sat a certain young man named Eutychus, who was sinking into a deep sleep. He was overcome by sleep; and as Paul continued speaking, he fell down from the third story and was taken up dead. But Paul went down, fell on him, and embracing him said, "Do not trouble yourselves, for his life is in him." Now when he had come up, had broken bread and eaten, and talked a long while, even till daybreak, he departed. And they brought the young man in alive, and they were not a little comforted.
(Acts 20:7–12)

Thus, with the unction of the Spirit upon him, Paul had gone down and fallen on the young man, embracing him in the power of the Spirit. Then Paul had returned and finished his message!

THE DAY OF PENTECOST

Now, in Acts 20:16, we find that the Day of Pentecost was near at hand. Again, what memories it had for Paul! We all look forward to observing Good Friday, when the cross of Calvary made an open door for all hearts to be saved; to commemorating Easter a few days later, when our Lord resurrected from the grave; and then to celebrating Whitsuntide or Pentecost and the wonderful descent of the Holy Spirit. When the Holy Spirit falls as He did at the beginning, He enlarges the hearts of all the people to live in the Spirit in such a way that there is new vision, new revelation, new equipping for service; new men are created. The baptism of the Holy Spirit means a new creation after the order of the Spirit.

INTERPRETATION OF TONGUES

For the Lord Himself descended by the power of the Spirit. "He shall not speak of Himself, and He will show you things to come." The baptism of the Holy Spirit is to fulfill in these bodies a new order—to everyone by a new power, to change from one state of grace to another—even by the Spirit of the Lord.

So Paul *"was hurrying to be at Jerusalem, if possible, on the Day of Pentecost"* (Acts 20:16). Understand, beloved, that many of the people at Jerusalem remembered the falling of the power as described in the second chapter of Acts.

There is a wonderful force of the anointing when all the people of God who are baptized with the Holy Spirit come together. What are religious conferences and conventions for? Their purpose is to meet the needs of those who are hungry and thirsty for God. Oh, this longing cry in the hearts of the people that can only be satisfied with more of God! On that memorable journey from Jerusalem to Damascus, Paul saw the risen Christ, and by the anointing of the Spirit, he became the greatest missionary the world has ever seen.

Oh, yes! There is something in unity, there is something in fellowship, there is something in being of one accord! Is the church today at such a place to receive? No! But God is in such a place to give. Who to? Only to thirsty, hungry souls. He has promised to fill *"the hungry with good things"* (Luke 1:53), and thus it will always be.

Now, what is the nature of a religious conference such as we are attending? It is a condition of not falling asleep, of not being lazy or apathetic; it is a condition of continual longing after God for a real outpouring of His Spirit. So Paul hurried to be at Jerusalem on the Day of Pentecost. Paul and the other believers expected wonderful things when they were once more in the Upper Room.

What was the plan as the disciples gathered together there? It was for preaching and telling the marvelous things that had happened.

> *Eye has not seen, nor ear heard, nor have entered into the heart of man the things which God has prepared for those who love Him. But God has revealed them to us through His Spirit.*
> (1 Cor. 2:9–10)

The Holy Spirit is revealing and strengthening continually. This has been so from Pentecost on up until the present day.

An old man once stood up in a meeting and was referring to one person and then another who had passed on. He said, "All the good people are gone now." Another brother stood up and exclaimed, "Thank God, that's a lie!" Oh, yes! There are lots of people on the earth today who have seen Jesus.

Jesus, by the power of the Holy Spirit, is making me understand that we are only still in the beginnings of Pentecost. Get back to Pentecost. Remain in the anointing. Paul was hurrying to be at

Jerusalem on the Day of Pentecost. Pentecost is the place where God can bestow such a measure of His love without limit, *"for God does not give the Spirit by measure"* (John 3:34).

A SEPARATING FORCE

The baptism of the Holy Spirit is not only the great essential power for victorious life and service, but it is also a separating force. Jesus said that a man's foes would often be those of his own household (Matt. 10:36). It means separation, as sure as you live, if you follow the narrow way that leads to life (Matt. 7:14). It means persecution, but if you follow wholly, you will have no room for anything but Jesus. You will be bound in the Spirit, led on, on, on:

> *And see, now I go bound in the spirit to Jerusalem, not knowing the things that will happen to me there, except that the Holy Spirit testifies in every city, saying that chains and tribulations await me. But none of these things move me; nor do I count my life dear to myself, so that I may finish my race with joy, and the ministry which I received from the Lord Jesus, to testify to the gospel of the grace of God.* (Acts 20:22–24)

Another side of this is that the world narrows to you. There are thousands of believers who mean well, but who do not see the need of the baptism of the Holy Spirit. So, in the first place, the old group has no room for you, but in the second place, the Holy Spirit binds you. You have no room, only to go the way of the Spirit in conformity to the will of God; you are bound to go the narrow way.

I have never seen the Holy Spirit change His position: His way leads to simplicity in living, nonconformity to the world. You will not find God beginning in the Spirit and leading back to the flesh. Do you have no liberty to go back? If you want to turn back, ask yourself where you are going. What did Paul say? "I go bound in the Spirit to Jerusalem's bonds and afflictions." (See Acts 20:22–23.) He added,

> *None of these things move me; nor do I count my life dear to myself, so that I may finish my race with joy, and the ministry which I received from the Lord Jesus, to testify to the gospel of the grace of God.*   (Acts 20:24)

The way—the way of the cross—is separation from the flesh, nonconformity to the world, but with an ever deepening and enlarging in that abounding fullness of life that flows from the throne of God.

You must be in the right place spiritually in order to see *"Him who is invisible"* (Heb. 11:27). Your mind must be operated by the Spirit, your desires under the control of the Spirit, and your plans directed and focused by the Spirit. (See Daniel 10.) Then, corruption is turned into comeliness. Then, your life in Christ becomes a wonderfully broad way, very broad, a perfection of complete orderliness. This is a state of being totally entrenched in the living God, bound in the Spirit! Can we take it in? There are depths we cannot fathom. I know it means bonds and afflictions (Acts 20:23 KJV). Shall I draw back? I cannot. Do you not see in Paul's willingness Jesus in a new form, Jesus again on the earth? This is the way we are bound to go. Paul called himself the *"bondservant"* of Jesus Christ. (See, for example, Romans 1:1.) But we are not obliged to be this! We could abandon our faith! Could I? Yes, I could! But I cannot! Separated bondservant, you cannot go back. It costs much to come, but it costs a thousand times more to retreat.

Oh, it's a costly thing to follow Jesus. Once having tasted the hidden manna, once having seen His face, it costs you your life to leave. (See Hebrews 6:4–6.) As Peter said, *"Lord, to whom shall we go? You have the words of eternal life"* (John 6:68).

INTERPRETATION OF TONGUES

The Lord is that Spirit, which has not only come in, but has embraced you and called you truly in the Spirit, that you might be a choice virgin betrothed to another, even Christ.

DEVOTED HEARTS

Shall we leave? No! Do you want to be unclothed? What a dreadful thing to be publicly exposed. (See Revelation 3:18.) What is it to be naked? To have a name for yourself! To be! And yet not to be! Lord, save us. Oh, for hearts that throb after the divine call. I love my Master. I do not want to be set free from serving Him. (See Exodus 21:5–6.)

This is no mediocre meeting; the Holy Spirit gently falls upon us. The Spirit of the living God yearns over us with tender compassion. God the Holy Spirit overshadows us. Some may say, "I want to get so near! I'll pay any price to come into this holy place!" Dear ones, you cannot take off your filthy garments. Christ unclothes your unrighteousness, and then He clothes you with the Holy Spirit! Oh, breathe every breath in the Holy Spirit. The old is taken away and the new is brought in, so that we never lose the fragrance of the divine presence, so that we fan and fan and fan until the Holy Spirit makes us living flames of fire carrying salvation everywhere, healing everywhere, the baptism of the Holy Spirit everywhere—on fire, bound forever, God thrilling the life.

INTERPRETATION OF TONGUES

It is the Lord Himself who has the choice of my heart, pruning to bring forth to His glory an eternal harvest gathered in forever.

There is something beautiful in the gift of tongues with interpretation, a joyfulness in experience—a sweet harmony establishing, fortifying, and making our hearts strong in Himself. The day is not far distant when we may have to stand very firm in what God is taking us on to. War, pestilence, famine— the order has not been altered since the world began. These are trying times for the believer. The world wants less of God and there is a great deal of trial of faith. Are we going to be found faithful? Two things will help you: faith and the baptism of the Holy Spirit. These will establish you against attacks or evil winds from any source.

We ought to be so established that we are ready and willing to be tried when the day comes, no matter which side the Spirit presses. There is always the thought that Jesus may come before that day, so that one is as likely as the other. God will strengthen your heart in the trial, in the evil day. He will never leave His own. Every man burned at the stake for the faith has been a seed, a light, a torch, bringing in a new order. Let us keep the vision clear—pure in heart, upward, onward, heavenward—*"until the day breaks and the shadows flee away"* (Song 2:17).

Jesus is the loveliest on earth. The Holy Spirit clothes Him. He met the need of all. You belong to the *"church of the firstborn"* (Heb. 12:23), the establishment of that wonderful place in the glory. Will you promise God that nothing will come between you and the throne—the heart of God and the mind of the Spirit? God has a choice for everyone *"who swears to his own hurt and does not change"* (Ps. 15:4)—a pressing right in.

Is my Jesus not beautiful? Could anything cloud that brow? He has the joy of redemption for us. We go from victory to victory. Your faces are a picture of what they will be in glory. Let us be zealous, setting to our seals that God is true, until that day when we will abide with Him forever. *"Set your house in order"* (2 Kings 20:1); you must go God's way—follow Him. The building is going up. The top stone must be put on. Grace, grace be unto it.

7

DIVINE CHARGING: CHANGING OTHERS

If you will believe, you will see the salvation of God. Only believe. Faith brings us into the kingdom of God—out of a natural order and into a divine order with divine power for promotion, charged by the power of God, by Another greater than we, a divine order.

> He came to His own, and His own did not receive Him. But as many as received Him, to them He gave the right to become children of God, to those who believe in His name.
>
> (John 1:11–12)

Only believe. A man is in a great place when he has no one to turn to but God. With only God to help, we are in an excellent place; God will change the situation. *"Not I, but Christ"* (Gal. 2:20 KJV). There is a new divine order for us to come into, that divine place where God works the miracle. God waits for us to act. Some boilers are made to go off at a ten-pound pressure, some at a two hundred fifty-pound pressure, and others at a three hundred fifty-pound pressure. What pressure do you want to blow off? Only believe. All things are possible; only believe (Mark 9:23).

"You shall receive power when the Holy Spirit has come upon you" (Acts 1:8). What there is for us in this mighty baptism of the Holy Spirit! We can be so moved by God's power that the borough of Llanelly and the whole of South Wales will again feel the power of God—their great inheritance in Christ Jesus—and all will know that we have been with Jesus (Acts 4:13). It is a changing that is the result of a meeting. The same thing happened when people met with Jesus, and we are "bone of His bones and flesh of His flesh" (see Genesis 2:23), and He has given us of His Spirit, *"grace for grace"* (John 1:16). We are baptized by the same Spirit into one body (1 Cor. 12:13), *"partakers of the divine nature"* (2 Pet. 1:4), living in a divine changing, with our whole beings aflame with the same passion that Jesus had, for Jesus said in Acts 1:8, *"You shall receive power when the Holy Spirit has come upon you."*

Jesus said this just before He ascended into heaven. He was clothed with grace, and His last moments on earth were filled with the power of the Spirit. Through the Holy Spirit, Jesus gave grace to man, which was so truly manifested in Him, promising a power like He had. He was going, but the work had to continue. Those He left behind on earth were to be thus clothed, thus charged with divine power by the divine working of the Spirit.

Some have thought that this wonderful baptism in the Spirit would quiet down. It reminds me of one of the first locomotive engines. When Stephenson got it all ready, he was eager for his sister Mary to see it. When Mary saw it, she said, "John, it will never go. It will never go." Stephenson said to his sister, "Get in!" He pressed a button, and the engine went. Then she said, "Oh, John! Oh, John, it will never stop; it will never stop!"

We know that as we waited and prayed, it looked as if the baptism would never come. But it did come, and now we know that it will never stop. We had the sense to wait until it did come. But now, when I see people seeking the Holy Spirit—do you know, beloved, that I believe it is wrong to wait for the Holy Spirit? The Holy Spirit is waiting for us. The Holy Spirit has come, and He will not return until the church goes to be with her Lord forever. So when I see people waiting, I know something is wrong. The Holy Spirit is revealing uncleanness, judging, hardness of heart, all impurity. Until the process of cleansing is complete, the Holy Spirit cannot come. But when the body is clean, sanctified, Jesus delights to fill us with His Holy Spirit. I know that it will never stop; we are wholly God's in the process of cleansing. The Holy Spirit is preparing our bodies as temples for the Spirit, to be made like Jesus is.

INTERPRETATION OF TONGUES

"It is the will of God, even your sanctification," that you should be filled unto all the fullness of God like a bannered army clothed with Him. Dynamite flowing through, Trinity working in holy, mighty power within the human frame. God in divine order, meaning us to be swallowed up in Him—a new body, a new mind, a new tongue. "No man can tame the tongue," but God can change the whole body to a perfect position by the Holy Spirit. The Christ enthroned within: from that, a divine order, a divine cooperation. "You shall receive power, the Holy Spirit coming upon you" in His perfect, operative, divine adjustment, the Word of God causing, unfolding, the divine plan by the sanctification of the Spirit.

Here is the hallmark of the mystery of divine ability, which must come in our day in its fullness. *"Jesus went about doing good"* (Acts 10:38). God was in Him bodily, in all fullness (Col. 2:9). I see, I know, the divine order; we must press in to the fullness of it. We speak what we do know and testify of what we have seen (John 3:11), the Holy Spirit being our witness. I see with the Master in His royal robe of holiness an impregnation of love moving and acting in the present tense of divine power, an association to be imparted. *"You shall receive power"*—the Master was already in this power in Acts 1:8; the disciples had to come into it. We are in it, of it, unto it. You cannot get rid of it, once it is in you, this power divine.

God's power is a tremendous thing to be born into. It is a serious thing, once engrafted, to grieve the Holy Spirit. (See Ephesians 4:30; Romans 11:13–25.) The baptism of the Holy Spirit is a fearful place if we are not going on with God. Great is our conviction of sin. The Holy Spirit comes to abide. God must awaken us to our responsibility, an inbreathed life of power. We can never be the same after the Holy Spirit has come upon us. We must *"be ready in season and out of season"* (2 Tim. 4:2), full of the Spirit, always abounding, always full of the life of God, ready for every emergency.

IN A GREATER PLACE

I know the Lord's laid His hand on me,

I know the Lord's laid His hand on me.

He filled me with the Holy Spirit;

I know the Lord's laid His hand on me.

I am always, always, in a place greater than the need of the situation. The baptism of the Holy Spirit is to prepare us for acting when two ways meet— where only God can give decision and bring off the victory, and where you stand still and see the salvation of God (Exod. 14:13). It's a great place to reach such a position of dignity, to be able to shout when the walls are up, when it looks as if all would fail. Shout! Shout! The victory is yours. Yes, the victory is yours. It is not to come at some future time. The victory is yours. Just as you shout, the ensign will arise and the walls will fall down, and you will walk in and possess the city. (See Joshua 6:1–20.)

It's a designed position; it is not of our making. It's a rising position, honoring the cry of the Master, *"It is finished!"* (John 19:30). It is not "to be finished," but *"It is finished!"* God can make that position manifest as I am in allegiance with His divine purposes. It is no little thing to be baptized with the Holy Spirit and to be saved from the power of Satan unto God. It is a greater thing than moving Mount Sinai to change a nature from an earthly position to a heavenly desire.

Jesus was in perfect order. He *"began both to do and teach"* (Acts 1:1, emphasis added). He began to be. He lived in a certain knowledge. We must allow God to work through us. God has declared it: we must be living epistles of Christ (2 Cor. 3:3), *"known and read by all men"* (v. 2). To be known, to have knowledge, His Word abiding in our hearts—a word of activity, a word of power, the power we have received, the Holy Spirit coming upon us, making us witnesses in Jerusalem, Judea, Samaria, and the uttermost parts of the earth (Acts 1:8).

A COMPASSION THAT DOES NOT FAIL

One morning, very early, I was traveling on a train in Sweden. An old lady came into the railway coach leaning on her daughter's arm. When I saw her sit down, with her face so full of anguish, I was disturbed. I could not rest. I am pursuing a course: how to get into the kingdom of the Master. Christ gives us a compassion that does not fail, that sees when no one else sees, that feels when no one else feels. It is a divine compassion; it comes by the Word, for He is the Word of God. We are balanced on God's side according to our faith, as our faith is embodied in the Master. *"Who is he who overcomes the world, but he who believes that Jesus is the Son of God [the Christ]?"* (1 John 5:5). Our life is in Another, associated with Another. He takes the lead through us—we live only for Him, and He extends Himself through us.

I said to my interpreter, "What is the cause of that woman's trouble? Will you find out?" The dear old lady said, "I am over seventy. I had hoped to keep my entire body until I died, but gangrene has set into my legs, and I am on my way to the hospital to have my legs amputated; the pain is terrible. I do not want to have my legs off at my age." I was bound to tell her that Jesus could heal. Her face lit up, her eyes sparkled, and she became radiant with hope. Then the train stopped and the coach filled up with workmen who stood between me and the woman. It looked hopeless for further talk. A big man stood between us. The Devil said, "Now you are done." Jesus knew how to answer the Devil. He answered him with the Word of God. The Devil may leave a dead fish but not a live one. The Devil said, "Now you are done." I said, "No! My Lord will make a way." Just then, the big man stretched his legs out. I put my hand on the woman and said, "In the name of Jesus, I bind and loose this woman." The man did not know why, but God knew. In that moment, she was healed.

What is my purpose in telling this story? *"You shall receive power when the Holy Spirit has come upon you"* (Acts 1:8). Jesus was clothed with power and with a ministry of imparting the power emblematic of divinity with an installation that never failed: the power to breathe in life and to scatter the power of the Enemy, *"and nothing shall by any means hurt you"* (Luke 10:19). When the train stopped, the old lady began to get out of the coach. The daughter said, "Why, Mother!" The lady said, "I am going back home. I am healed." As long as the train stood, she walked up and down past the window of the coach. She said to the interpreter, "I am going home. I am healed."

He'll never forget to keep me,

He'll never forget to keep me;

My Father has many dear children,

But He'll never forget to keep me.

God will not allow those who trust in Him to become failures in the difficult places of life. God does the work. Yes, He does. This Word is a living Word of divine activity with momentum. It has power to change the nature by the power of the Spirit. All disease and weakness must go at the rebuke of the Master. God enables us to bind the Enemy and set the captive free. Beloved, arise, *"the glory of the LORD is risen upon you"* (Isa. 60:1), pouring life into your weakness, making you *"the head and not the tail"* (Deut. 28:13).

This is a wonderful day, filled with the Spirit. The breath of the Almighty, God the Holy Spirit, can take the Word of Jesus and breathe a quickened spirit into those who hear it. Jesus began to do, then to teach (Acts 1:1). You are in a divine process with revelation and divine power in the place of manifestation. If I come only to impart the life that has brought revelation, God will be with me and blessing will flow.

One day, in San Francisco, on a busy streetcar route, I saw a great crowd. I asked the driver to stop. I saw a boy lying in the agony of death, and I said, "What is it, boy?" He answered in a breathy voice, "Cramp." There was no time to pray. Only time to act! I see Acts 1:8, *"You shall receive power."* It's the divine order: fire burning, power flowing, divine glory. Getting my hand around the boy, I said, "Come out!" The boy jumped up and ran off—never even saying thank you.

Another day, on board ship, I had risen early and was on deck. I saw my table steward, but he did not see me. He seemed to be in great pain. I heard him say, "Oh, I cannot bear it. What will I do?" I jumped up and said, "Come out!" He said, "What is it?" I said, "It's God." He had hurt his back lifting a heavy weight, but God healed him.

Yes, beloved, we have an almighty God who is able to help, able to comfort—the *"God of all comfort"* (2 Cor. 1:3).

The Holy Spirit has come upon you with the power of impartation to a needy world. Act, for you have received power, the power of changing. Thus God is glorified, and the needs of the needy are met. Power is received, the unction goes forth, and God is glorified. Receiving the power, let the rivers flow (John 7:37–38). Amen.

8

EPISTLES OF CHRIST

All thoughts of holiness are God's; all manner of loving-kindness and tender mercies are His. All weaknesses are made for us so that we might be in a place of absolute helplessness, for when we are weak, then we are strong (2 Cor. 12:10). All divine acquaintance with Him today will put us in the place where we may be the broken, empty vessel, ready for Christ's use. (See 2 Timothy 2:20–21.)

"Whom have I in heaven but You? And there is none upon earth that I desire besides You" (Ps. 73:25). Oh, that is a wonderful place, where all your springs are in Him (Ps. 87:7), all your desires are after Him, and you long only for Him!

Get ready, so that you may be touched by His inward earnestness, so that you may see the power of possibility in an impossible place, until you see that God can change you until you will change other things, until you see today that your song will remain in flight.

Are you ready? You may ask, "What for?" For God to be all in all, and for you to lose your identity in the perfection of His glorified purity—for you to be lost to everything else except Him.

Are you ready? What for? For you to come to the banquet house with a great faith—nothing stopping you—pressing into, laying hold of, believing all things. You will have a time of great refreshing as you come expressing yourself to God.

We must not stop this holy pursuit. We must remember that whatever happens in these days is happening for our future benefit. If it deals with the flesh, with the carnal senses at all, and with the human spirit, it is because God has to have the right-of-way in our lives.

In 2 Corinthians 3, we have a very blessed word. If you get this truth into your heart, you will not be shaken anymore by anything. This is precisely the difference between the human and the divine. If the human is there prominently, then divine vision will be dimmed. When the divine has full control, then all earthly cares and anxieties pass away. If we live in the Spirit, we live above all human, animal nature. If we reach the climax that God's Son said we had to come into, we will always be in the place of peace.

"If you abide in Me, and My words abide in you, you will ask what you desire, and it shall be done for you" (John 15:7).

Jesus was a manifestation of power to dethrone every evil thing, and He always dealt with the flesh. It was necessary for Him to say to Peter, *"Get behind Me, Satan! You are an offense to Me, for you are not mindful of the things of God, but the things of men"* (Matt. 16:23). Everything that interferes with your plan of putting to death the *"old man"* (Eph. 4:22) is surely the old man that is comforting you.

There is a rest of faith if we have entered into it, if we have "*ceased from* [our] *own works*" (Heb. 4:10 KJV), ceased from our own struggling, ceased from making our own plans. It is a rest in faith, a place where you can smile in the face of any disruption. No matter what comes, you will be in the place of real rest. This may be seen in 2 Corinthians:

> *Do we begin again to commend ourselves? Or do we need, as some others, epistles of commendation to you or letters of commendation from you? You are our epistle written in our hearts, known and read by all men; clearly you are an epistle of Christ, ministered by us, written not with ink but by the Spirit of the living God, not on tablets of stone but on tablets of flesh, that is, of the heart.*   (2 Cor. 3:1–3)

Here we have a very remarkable word that the Spirit wants to enlarge upon for us. It is true that we must be the *"epistle of Christ."* The epistle of Christ is a living power in the mortal flesh, making alive, and dividing asunder everything that is not of the Spirit, until you realize that you now live in a new order. It is the Spirit who has manifested Himself in your mortal body. The Word has become life; it has quickened you throughout, and you are not in any way subject to anything around you. You are above everything; you reign above everything.

You are clearly sent forth by the Word of God as the epistle of Christ. By this I mean that all human ideals, plans, and wishes for the future are past. For you, *"to live is Christ"* (Phil. 1:21). For you, to live is to be His epistle, emblematic, divinely sustained by another power greater than you. So you do not seek your own anymore; you are living in a place where God is on the throne, superintending your human life. God is changing everything and making you understand this wonderful truth.

I believe it would be good to read just a little passage from the next chapter:

> *For it is the God who commanded light to shine out of darkness, who has shone in our hearts to give the light of the knowledge of the glory of God in the face of Jesus Christ. But we have this treasure in earthen vessels, that the excellence of the power may be of God and not of us.* (2 Cor. 4:6–7)

This is *"the excellence of the power"* of the life of Christ in the mortal body, subduing it in every way until the body is full of the life and vitality of the Spirit, so that Christ, God, and the Holy Spirit may be illuminating the whole body. The body is there just as the temple, so that all the glory should roll back to God. You are not seeking your own, not seeking your place, but your whole body is giving place to the glorifying of the Christ. You are set free by, loosed by, created by, and made like Him in this glorious order.

NOT LIVING UNDER THE LAW

If you go back into the law at any time and under any circumstances, you miss the divine order of the Spirit. You do not have to go back to the law. You are in a new order. Law can only deal out one thing, and I will read what it deals out in Hebrews 7:16: *"Not after the law of a carnal commandment, but after the power of an endless life"* (KJV). You never deal with law without finding that it is *"a carnal commandment,"* always dealing with carnal things. It is always "Thou shalt not."

There is no law to the Spirit; there never has been. You cannot find a law to Truth. The law has never had a place in a human body that has been filled with the power and the unction of the Holy Spirit. Law is done away with, law is past; life is begun, the new creation is formed, living after the new order. Christ has become the very principle of your human life, and you no longer touch law. You are above the law.

How many people are missing the greatest plan of the earth because they are continually trying to *do* something? Many years ago, my wife and I were strongly convinced along Sabbath Day holiness lines. We got so far that we thought it was wrong to have the milkman deliver on Sundays. We felt that it was a very fearful thing to ride in any vehicle on a Sunday. We were so tightened up by the law that we were bound hand and foot.

There are thousands of people like that today. There are people who are taking up the new order of what they call the Seventh-day Adventists. But I want to tell you, you are dealing with miry clay when you deal with anything regarding eating or drinking, or anything pertaining to the law. (See Colossians 2:16–17, 20–23.)

God wants you in a new order. It is *"the law of the Spirit"* (Rom. 8:2). It is a law of life. It is not a law of death and bondage. (See verse 2.)

As sure as you are in law, you are in judgment, and you judge everybody. Law is always judgment, and no one is right except those people who are keeping the law. They are full of judgment. But we have passed from death, from judgment, from criticism, from harshness, from hardness of heart.

You are our epistle,...known and read by all men....And we have such trust through Christ toward God. Not that we are

*sufficient of ourselves to think of anything as being from our-
selves, but our sufficiency is from God.*   (2 Cor. 3:2, 4–5)

Every person who begins thinking anything about himself is
dealing with human weakness. When you in any way try to please
anybody, you are down. And you are down very low if you begin to
worship anybody. No person must be worshipped.

When the glory appeared on the Mount of Transfiguration, as
soon as it appeared and the disciples saw the whiteness, the brilliancy, the glory, the expression of the Master, and the very robes He
wore becoming white and glistening, they began at once to think of
what they could do. Law will do this. It asks, "What can we *do?*" So
the disciples began doing; they wanted to make three tabernacles:
one for Moses, one for Elijah, and one for Jesus. And then the cloud
came. When the cloud lifted, no one was seen but Jesus. No person
in the world must be worshipped but the Lord. (See Matthew
17:1–8.)

If you turn to anybody but Jesus, you will be law, you will be
carnal nature, you will be human. This has always been so. People
are always figuring out things to do. They ask, "What can I do?"
That is the reason why in the fourth chapter of Romans we read
that the man who begins to do is a debtor to what he does; but for
the man who believes God, it is counted to him for righteousness. It
is not doing, but believing (Rom. 4:3–5). So God wants you to see
that you have to cease from your own doing (Heb. 4:10), to get away
from it. Believe that there is a spiritual vitality that will bring into
your very nature a new creation, which must be in the sons of God
with power.

INTERPRETATION OF TONGUES

"It is the Light that lights everyone who comes into the world." It is the purity of the Son of God that is to bring us into a place where we will behold light in His light. It is the revelation from the Most High God, for "in the old days men spoke as the prophets, but now in the last days God speaks to us by His Son." His Son is in evidence, not the prophets but the Son. But if the prophets speak, as it will be, concerning the Son, then you will find that the prophet position will be Amen to the Word of God.

Who also made us sufficient as ministers of the new covenant, not of the letter but of the Spirit; for the letter kills, but the Spirit gives life. (2 Cor. 3:6)

In this new order, Jesus has one great plan for us: to fill us with the Holy Spirit so that He will have a perfect focus in our human life, making all the displays of the brilliancy centered around the Son. And as we come into the light of this revelation by the Son, by the quickening of the Spirit, we will find our whole body regenerated with a new touch of divine favor, and we will think about spiritual things, and we will talk about spiritual things, and we will not touch anything that pertains to the flesh.

INTERPRETATION OF TONGUES

It is the Light that dawns just in the early morning and sets your soul aglow with the fervent heat of the light of the revelation of the Son. "For whom He loves, He corrects" and changes, and brings him to a desired heaven.

I love the dawning of the morning, breaking upon my soul with refreshing and keeping me in perfect order!

THE SPIRIT OR THE LETTER?

"The letter kills, but the Spirit gives life" (2 Cor. 3:6). Think about this very sincerely. Many people go along very well for a time in the Spirit, and then they go back to the law.

We have no trouble with people who are getting baptized or seeking the baptism or right when the Holy Spirit has touched them. All those positions are lovely. When are we troubled? When people cease to pursue God and they turn aside and spoil all that has been before. What has happened? They were all right in the pursuit of God, and they would have been all right continuing in the pursuit. But they turned aside.

There is not a place in the Scripture where you are ever allowed to drop the weapons of spiritual attainment. You must see that you must denounce the powers of evil, the powers of darkness, the powers that would bring you into bondage. Denounce them all. You have been created now, filled now, sustained in power. Go right on with God; never turn again to the things around you. Set your heart only upon Him, just as Jesus set His heart upon the cross.
There are three things that are wonderful. There is a good, there is a better, and there is a best.

After you have come into the fullness of the refreshing of God, it is possible to look to the letter instead of to the spirit, or the life, of the Word. The letter will turn you to yourself, but the spirit will turn you to Christ.

I say this without flinching: those who have turned to baptizing people in water in Jesus' name only, rather than in the name of the

Father, Son, and Holy Spirit, have turned away from a higher order of God. The people who have changed from baptism in the name of the Trinity to baptism in the name of Jesus only have turned away from the best; they have "good"—but that is all they have.

But there is a best. What is it? It is not the spirit but the letter of the law that kills. People turn away from the spirit and take the letter, and when they get in the letter, they are full of condemnation. If they had gone on with God, the Spirit would have kept them in life. As you live in the Spirit, there will be no condemnation in you. There is something wrong when you are the only one who is right. As the church rises into the glory of the Lord and the vision of the Lord, she will be full of the love of the Lord.

The Holy Spirit wants you to sweep through darkness. The Holy Spirit wants to fill you with truth. The Holy Spirit wants to stimulate you in liberty. The Holy Spirit wants you to rise higher and higher.

What does the Devil do? He tries to get you to believe that you have some special revelation—some special revelation that is actually only partial truth. The Devil never gives whole truth; he always gives partial truth. What did the Devil say to Jesus? "*If You are the Son of God…*" (Matt. 4:3, emphasis added). The Devil knew that He was the Son of God.

I hear that there is a place in Los Angeles where they spend all their time speaking in tongues, to the exclusion of anything else. How ridiculous! How foolish! What's going on? It's the letter of the law, a turning away from the real truth of the Word of God.

God will shake this thing through you. If you turn away from the Word of God and won't have the Word, you will be judged by the Word of God and you will be brought into leanness.

Spiritual power will not have human attainment. The man who is living in the Spirit will not turn aside to please anybody. The man who is filled with the Spirit is going on with God all the time, and he will cease from his own works (Heb. 4:10).

I want to save you from getting into ruts. I want to stir your holy fidelity to know that there is a place in the Holy Spirit that can keep you so that you do not get hard in the law, in judgment, in criticism, in hardness of heart. Get to where the Spirit has such a place with you that you will love to go God's way.

The judgment of God will begin at the house of God (1 Pet. 4:17).

You have the best when you have the Spirit, and the Spirit brings life and revelation. Don't turn to the law; don't turn to the natural. See to it that in the spiritual you are free from the law. The law of the Spirit is life, to keep you out of death, to keep you out of judgment, to keep you out of bondage (Rom. 8:2).

When Moses knew that he was bringing the tablets of stone with the commandments down to the Israelite people, his heart was so full of joy, his whole body was so full, his whole countenance was so full that the people could not look upon him because of the glory that was expressed in his face. (See Exodus 34.) What was it? He was bringing liberty to the people—and it was law.

> *But if the ministry of death, written and engraved on stones, was glorious, so that the children of Israel could not look steadily at the face of Moses because of the glory of his countenance, which glory was passing away, how will the ministry of the Spirit not be more glorious?* (2 Cor. 3:7–8)

If the law, which had with it life and revelation and blessing for Israel, could bring that wonderful exhibition of beauty and glory, what is it, then, if we are freed from the law and have the Spirit living and moving in us, without harshness, without "Thou shalt nots," the Spirit of the Lord breathing through us and making us *"free from the law of sin and death"* (Rom. 8:2)? Let us see to it that we get there.

For a moment, I want to talk to you about the body. There are people who want to be loosed in their minds, in their bodies, from their afflictions, loosed in every way.

You will never get loosed in the flesh; you will never get loosed in the letter. You will only get loosed as the Spirit of the Lord breathes upon the Word and you receive it as life from the Lord, for the Word of the Lord is life. Receive the Word of the Lord just as it is and believe it, and you will find that it gives life to your whole body.

Any number of people are missing it because they are full of examination. You have to take the Word of God as the life of the Spirit, and you have to allow it to breathe through you, giving life to your whole body; for the Spirit gives life but the flesh profits nothing (John 6:63).

The Word may be quick and powerful, or it may be deathlike. *God wants us to be through with death.* You are to be through with death as far as the law is concerned. But you are to die to yourself and remain in this death until death is swallowed up by the perfect victory of the perfect resurrection of the life of the Spirit that moves in you, giving life to your mortal body. The very moment that you turn from the spiritual health of this revelation of Christ, you have ceased to go forward.

A man came to one of my meetings. He was a Wesleyan minister, and he was wonderfully blessed. He groaned, he travailed, he paid the price. Every time the Spirit came in, he went down and down and down into real death, and God quickened him by the Spirit. So forcefully, so powerfully did the Spirit of the Lord breathe upon him that he became like a flame of fire. He was in Vancouver. Every place became too small; every place became completely filled. Money flowed in, thousands of dollars. Oh, the glory! The people of Vancouver, looking at this young man, felt the glory, the expression of God flowing through his face; it was so beautiful.

However, he was turned aside to baptizing in the name of Jesus only. His glory departed. He lost everything he had and then was shoved into a small theater. He lost everything.

What caused it? Going back to the letter, missing the summit, the glory that was upon him.

He wept and wept and wept and said, "How can I get back?"

"Repent, brother," I said. "Repent."

Some people are always covering the thing up when they know they are wrong; they won't repent. If you have gone off the line and have gone the wrong way because people have said to go that way, if you have left the *"first principles"* (Heb. 5:12) of the Christ of God, why not repent and get right with God? And I heard that this man from Vancouver had repented.

(Interruption from the balcony: "Yes, he has, Brother Wigglesworth, and he has gotten the victory, too, praise God!")

Oh, that is the man! God will restore everything to you. When we repent, God restores.

INTERPRETATION OF TONGUES

It is of the depths and where you cannot trace and wonders come, and in the mystery of the wonderment where two ways meet and your heart cries and even your nakedness appears in such a way that you do not know; then in your lowliness you turn again to the habitation of the Spirit, and the Lord "turns your captivity" and "heals your lands," and restores again to you the vineyard and opens the heavens upon you for blessing.

Oh, I see young men come into this work, I see people come into this work, and I know it is like opening the greatest door! Oh, what can happen! I see men graduating from colleges; I see men clothed with great abilities! Oh, how God can move them!

If I never went to school, if my mother and father never could read and write, and if my wife taught me to read, then I come to you just because the Holy Spirit has got my life; I come to you to help you. But what can happen to a man who has been *"at the feet of Gamaliel"* (Acts 22:3) and has touched all the fullness of the fragrance of knowledge? What God could do if you would let Him! Will you let Him?

You began well; what has hindered you? (Gal. 5:7). Was it the Lord who came in the way? No, the Lord never stops your progress. It was some human thing. There was something that glittered, but it was not pure gold. There was something that shook your confidence, but it was never God.

Therefore, I pray for you, you mighty of the Lord, you children of the Most High God, you people whom the Lord is looking upon with great favor. Believe that as the Holy Spirit moved upon Paul, moved upon the apostles, He can bring you forth, tried as gold and purified (Job 23:10).

Will you believe? May the blessing of God—the Father, the Son, and the Holy Spirit—fill you so that all the powers of hell will not be able to prevail against you (Matt. 16:18).

I had no idea of what was going to happen this morning, but I do praise God. There has risen in my heart such love for this brother who repented. I have wept alone, very sorry, troubled, wondering what would be the outcome of it. I got three men to pray with me so that we might bind the powers, so that he might be loosed. He does not know anything about it. My daughter and I have gone before the Lord for him.

Oh, I do hope that the future will be very mighty! Let us pray that God will send him to Vancouver with this new thrill of holy life pressing through, until Vancouver will feel the warmth of heaven!

O God, we pray you, bless this dear soul. He has been heartbroken for so long. He has been in great stress and trial for so long. O God, let the Holy Spirit rest upon him and move him for Vancouver, and let no power in the world interfere with his progress. In Jesus' name.

THE GLORY SIDE

Now it is the glory side that I am coming to. I want you to notice that there is an exceeding glory, and it is only in the knowledge of the Lord Jesus:

> But if the ministry of death, written and engraved on stones, was glorious, so that the children of Israel could not look steadily at the face of Moses because of the glory of his countenance,

which glory was passing away, how will the ministry of the Spirit not be more glorious? For if the ministry of condemnation had glory, the ministry of righteousness exceeds much more in glory. For even what was made glorious had no glory in this respect, because of the glory that excels. For if what is passing away was glorious, what remains is much more glorious. (2 Cor. 3:7–11)

"*Which glory was passing away*" (v. 7). Was it ever thought possible that the law could pass away? Yes, by something that is far more glorious.

There were three things in the old dispensation that were far different from four things in the new dispensation. Let us start by looking at the old dispensation. First, in the Old Testament, we read, "*What does the* LORD *require of you but to do justly?*" (Mic. 6:8).

"Doing justly" is something that the law was continually confronting the people of the Old Testament with. Everybody was out of order, and so the God of Almightiness drew them to the place where the first thing necessary for them to know was how to "*do justly.*"

Second, we read, "*What does the* LORD *require of you but to... love mercy?*" (v. 8). In the law, they had no mercy, and God brought this right into the midst of the law, a thing that they did not know how to do.

Third, we read, "*What does the* LORD *require of you but to... walk humbly with your God?*" (v. 8). The person who keeps the law through his own efforts never walks humbly, but is always filled with self- righteousness.

But now let the Spirit speak to us in the last days. What is it that the Lord your God desires of you?

First, in the New Testament, we read, *"You shall love the* LORD *your God with all your heart"* (Mark 12:30). Isn't that a new spiritual vision? That isn't the law; that is a boundless position. Law could never do it.

Second, we read, *"You shall love the* LORD *your God with all your...soul"* (v. 30). Third, we read, *"You shall love the* LORD *your God with all your...mind"* (v. 30)—with all of your pure mind, serving the Lord.

Fourth, we read, *"You shall love the* LORD *your God with all your...strength"* (v. 30). No holding back.

The law had to pass away because, although it was glorious, the ministry of the Spirit was exceeding in glory. God's people could now serve Him with a pure heart, giving all their strength for God.

Just imagine your knowing that you are so created after the fashion of God that you need all the strength you receive from your food for God—all the strength. Just imagine, you people who have wonderful capabilities and wonderful minds, your minds have to be all for God.

Glorious, more glorious! It is exceeding glory. Your own has to pass away. Nothing will put law away except perfect love. There is no law to love. Love never had a law; it never felt it was making a sacrifice. If you ever talk about sacrifice, it shows you do not know what it is to love.

"For the joy that was set before Him [Jesus] *endured the cross"* (Heb. 12:2). It is as if Christ Jesus said, "The cross is nothing to Me; death itself is nothing to Me. All that people do to Me is nothing. Oh, the joy I have in saving all the people of the world!"

Oh, the depth of the grace, of the majesty, of the holiness, of the sweetness!

> Oh, this is like heaven to me,
>> This is like heaven to me;
> I've crossed over Jordan to
>> Canaan's fair land,
> And this is like heaven to me.

If you are in this love, you will be swallowed up with holy desire; you will have no desire but the Lord. Your mind will be filled with divine reflection. Your whole heart will be taken up with the things that pertain to the kingdom of God, and you will live in *"the secret place of the Most High,"* and you will abide there (Ps. 91:1).

Remember, it is as you abide there that He covers you with His feathers (v. 4). It is the inmost place, where you have moved wholly away from earthly things, and where the Lord now has the treasures. (See Colossians 2:2–3.)

There is an exceeding glory; there is a glory where you forget your poverty, where you forget your weaknesses, where you forget your past human nature, and you go on to divine opportunity.

"For if the ministry of condemnation had glory, the ministry of righteousness exceeds much more in glory" (2 Cor. 3:9). You see, the law is a *"ministry of condemnation,"* and the Spirit is a *"ministry of righteousness."* The difference is this: instead of preaching "Thou shalt not" to the people any longer, you now preach that there is a superabundant position in the Holy One in the life of the Son, in the reflection by the Holy Spirit into the entirety of your whole heart, where He

has come in and transformed the whole situation until every judged thing is past, life flows through, and you preach righteousness.

You will never get free by keeping the law; but if you believe in the cleansing blood of Jesus, you will be dead to self and sin, you will have life divine, and you can sweep through the thing that binds you because righteousness will abound where the law is of the Spirit.

The Jews will never have this light revealed to them until one thing happens. What is happening now? I have talked with rabbis. I have good times with them; I visit the synagogues and see good things there, and I have good times with these people.

When I was in Jerusalem on a speaker's platform with a number of Jewish rabbis, I had a chance to talk about the law and freedom in the Spirit. I had been preaching at every place around there; I had preached in the prison. I tell you, it was lovely to preach at the foot of Mount Carmel. It was very lovely for me to wake up and look across the Sea of Galilee and see that place where the demons went into the pigs and ran down the hill. (See Luke 8:26–33.)

I had a good time there, but most glorious of all was that last address I gave for half an hour on a Jerusalem platform in front of all these judges, addressing these people from all over the country, as the power of God fell upon me, with tears running down my face, telling about the Nazarene, the King of Kings, the Lord of Glory, moving them to the Spirit instead of the law.

It was glorious. They came around me afterward, and several of these Jews and one of the rabbis rode with me in the train. Then, when we got to Alexandra, they went with me to have some food.

"There is something about your preaching that is different from the rabbi," they said.

"Well, what is it?" I asked.

"Oh, you moved us! There was a warmth about it!"

"Yes, brother," I said. "It wasn't law. The glory position is that it is warm—you feel it, it is regenerative, it is quickening, it moves your human nature, it makes you know that this is life divine."

Those around the table listened, and these Jews said, "Oh, but it is so different!"

"Yes," I said, "and the day is coming when your veil will be taken from your eyes and you will see this Messiah." (See 2 Corinthians 3:14–17.)

After dinner, they said, "We have to leave. Oh, we do not feel we want to leave you."

Oh, brothers and sisters, the Jews some day will be grafted in. (See Romans 11:17–24.) The day of the Jews is coming. But, oh, I don't want us Gentiles to miss the opportunity!

God wants us now so filled with the Spirit that we do not lose the glory by judging and harshness. We forget these things and we *"press toward the mark for the prize of the high calling of God in Christ Jesus"* (Phil. 3:14 KJV), and we see that we have received the life of the Spirit, which has quickened us, for *"where the Spirit of the Lord is, there is liberty"* (2 Cor. 3:17).

Liberty? What kind of liberty? Liberty *"from glory to glory"* (v. 18). The liberty that looses you, until the very affection of the nature of the Son of God begins to be, until you are absorbed in this glory.

What is man that You are mindful of him, and the son of man that You visit him? For You have made him a little lower than the angels, and You have crowned him with glory and honor.

(Ps. 8:4–5)

It is the Spirit that makes us alive; it is the Word that brings life. I want you to eat of the *"hidden manna"* (Rev. 2:17). I do not want you to eat the sour grapes that set your teeth on edge (Jer. 31:30). I want you to *"eat and be satisfied"* (Ps. 22:26)—to eat what is spiritual, life-giving, and divine.

9

THE FAVORED PLACE

Are you in? Oh, be in! Be in Christ, in God. To have union with God—to have direct communion with God with no other power interfering—is worth everything. It is a place of transmission of power, an ascent and descent of communication, charged by the divine operation of the Spirit. God gives us His outlook as we eat His flesh and drink His blood. (See John 6:53–58.) As Peter said, *"To whom* [else] *shall we go? You have the words of eternal life"* (v. 68).

INTERPRETATION OF TONGUES

Ready for action, moved by the breath of the Spirit—to pray through, to preach through, manifesting the glory of the Lord, having a double portion of the Spirit, bathed in ecstasy, delight, and joy. Your will done—each a perfect son.

You are in a favored place, a priceless position, if you have no way out, no where to go, but God. When Jesus said He is *"the true bread from heaven*" (v. 32), "*the bread of God*" (v. 33), that was the closest association with the revelation of what He is. The crowds still clung to Him as He spoke of that spiritual bread. They were fed from the depths, and they knew they had never had that before. They said, "*Lord, give us this bread always*" (John 6:34). It is not an earthly conception; it has no earthly roots—it is all divine, perfect, with no human oratory. God wants a people that He can feed with "*the finest of wheat*" (Ps. 81:16). For the harvest is fully ripe and ready to be gathered in. "*First the blade, then the ear, after that the full corn in the ear*" (Mark 4:28 KJV). It is ready to be gathered into the golden granary forever.

INTERPRETATION OF TONGUES

And "this bread is that which comes down." God gave the life of His Son, bestowing the true bread. He—the Lamb slain from the foundation of the world.

I beseech you therefore, brethren, by the mercies of God, that you present your bodies a living sacrifice, holy, acceptable to God, which is your reasonable service. And do not be conformed to this world, but be transformed by the renewing of your mind, that you may prove what is that good and acceptable and perfect will of God. (Rom. 12:1–2)

The breathing through of the divine character by the Spirit is priceless. There are no bounds. It enlarges and enlarges in our hands, just as the bread in the Master's hands did as He fed the five thousand. In the same way, today, the Bread is enlarging the child of God who can enter into this life-giving truth. He is held! Held! Held! He no longer holds God—God has hold of him! The Son has hold of him. The Holy Spirit has hold of him—has him. He is born of God. All things are overcome victoriously; things that are not of God fall away—manifesting how God is moving and changing you. You see the necessity that God be glorified, and you get rid of yourself. It is not an easy path.

Some people seem to be born good—goody-goody. I am of a different order. I speak from a human standpoint—the standpoint of weak, depraved humanity, but with a touch of heaven within to change it so that it is all-sufficient (2 Cor. 3:5–6). His blood, His touch, His grace does the work. It is not abundance of revelation, but the revelation of our own weaknesses, that brings about the change. The grace that comes in a time of extremity, meeting our need—that is the real messenger of possibility (2 Cor. 12:9). God takes everything, and from then on makes us channels of holiness, righteousness, and purity—wholly swallowed up in the life of the Spirit. This is inexpressible! It is life divine, joy, fullness.

Yesterday, I was interested in motorcycles. I was at the motor show. I was never so in the midst of something and out of it at the same time—never. I shouted, "Hallelujah!" and "Glory!" and all kinds of things to God. I could not fellowship with the motorcycles. I was in the motor show—but not of it. (See John 17:11, 14.) There is a new order above nature's plan, and it is the order of God. How beautifully God spoke this verse to me: *"I beseech you therefore, brethren, by the mercies of God, that you present your bodies a living sacrifice"* (Rom. 12:1).

Being a living sacrifice is not the end of sanctification—that has no end. It is not the end of the cleansing of the blood of Jesus. It is wholly a life proven. We are not saved more than once—but we are out of fellowship with God many times. Salvation is a being saved, a readiness to meet Jesus at any moment, a plan of increasing—a decreasing of self with an increasing Christlikeness (see John 3:30)—an enlarging to revelation so that we may manifest Him, making every time a progress in sanctification, the purification of our whole body. Our set purpose is to be transformed by the Holy Spirit (v. 2). This is the great order—a daily changing.

I am seeing the altar, the sacrifice—it is according to the mercies of God (v. 1). The living sacrifice was holy; it came to the place of acceptance with God. It is not complete, but God possesses it. God took the will and the whole desire, and He put them into His treasury of love and said, "I will accept the sacrifice," and He did. Oh, the joy of the knowledge that it will be complete! We are to be more helpless, more dependent on God. These are the ashes of the sacrifice. Every human power and human program fails. When we present our bodies as living sacrifices, there comes the bliss of the breath of the Spirit. Every divine inflow of the power of the Spirit is for an enlarging, bringing the soul into separation, into divine revelation, when God bends over and sweetly smiles, saying, "It is all right—only go further on, on, on!"

Oh, the joy of the knowledge. Paul spoke out of an offering, a sacrifice. You cannot speak out of anything else. All God's choice positions come out of an offering. Because Jesus offered Himself for us, God gave Him a name *"above every name"* (Phil. 2:9). Present your body as a living sacrifice—a whole offering. This does not mean that it will yet be a perfect sacrifice, but through calling us to be living sacrifices, God began a new plan of His great purpose.

So, "[God] *will rest in his love, he will joy over* [us] *with singing"* (Zeph. 3:17 KJV). He prepared the *"precious fruit"* for the flood time of the *"early"* and now the *"latter rain,"* for He is coming (James 5:7).

Do not be conformed to this world, but be transformed by the
renewing of your mind, that you may prove what is that good
and acceptable and perfect will of God.   (Rom. 12:2)

The baptism of the Holy Spirit is perfected: coming into those
who are helpless, investing with a force mightier than the human,
moving—knowing that the Greatest of all is there. The Holy Spirit
gets the great position: focusing all on the Son. The Holy Spirit
reveals the Son in you. You must decrease, and He must increase
(John 3:30). How? By the revelation of the Spirit.

There is no experience like that of the second chapter of Acts.
It is the greatest opportunity God has afforded to man. Submit to
Almighty God. The human spirit actually may be in great activity in
a person who has offered himself to God. Your "I" must be knocked
out and your personality must be fully surrendered to God. God
moves me to see that there is *"no good thing"* in me (Rom. 7:18 KJV).
No! You can polish up the *"old man"* (Rom. 6:6), but he is still the
old creation and worthless. Rise to the higher order of revelation
with God.

Jesus is the greatest of all, revealing and fulfilling divine activity.
He lives and moves in the world—and *"He learned obedience by the*
things which He suffered" (Heb. 5:8). He did not come to do His own
will. He lived freely, and the Father could enact His will through
Him.

There was nothing in the flesh; it was weak (Rom. 8:3). But God
"[sent] *His own Son in the likeness of sinful flesh, on account of sin: He*
condemned sin in the flesh" (v. 3). This glorious Son spoke and acted,
bringing divine revelation to us through the breath of the Spirit,
saying, *"Do not be conformed to this world, but be transformed,"* so that
you may prove, see, and know the *"perfect will of God"* (Rom. 12:2).

INTERPRETATION OF TONGUES

Forever the King reigns when the body is yielded. The will conforms by the power of the Son of God through the Spirit.

He lives and reigns forever, and by His grace we will reign forever with Him (2 Tim. 2:12), living with the King. It is worth a thousand deaths to come into one life. Even if we have failed a thousand times, God can fan and fan and fan our lives until the smoking flax is ablaze (Isa. 42:3) with divine equipment and a divine association.

I know the Lord's laid His hand on me,

I know the Lord's laid His hand on me.

He filled me with the Holy Spirit;

I know the Lord's laid His hand on me.

Praise the Lord. Beloved, God had more in mind than the necessity of changing us. He had in mind the fullness of the Holy Spirit, gifts, graces, the rarities of heaven dawning upon us, being wholly separated unto God forever, all spiritual revelation and power coming within the body, bringing joy and help to others—all these things working through and without.

I have travailed. I know nothing about giving birth, but I know about travailing with God and laboring until God brings forth the process of His inward working. All heaven's rays focus until the body seems too small to contain what is coming in.

We must understand the breath of the Spirit, the breath of God. We were born to yield. We must know when to begin and when to stop—to be at all times a perfect channel for the breath of the Spirit of God. All of this is a perfect blending of Trinity divine to keep us in the place where God wants us all the time, having a mind of reflection.

The reflection of the mind always produces the operation of the tongue. In the sanctity of the Spirit, we are not conformed to the world but are transformed by the renewing of our minds. Your mind is not to focus on earthly things, but is to be shorn of earthly desire; it is to be in a supernatural order, filled with illumination. For Acts 1:8 says, *"You shall receive power"*—not power by the Holy Spirit, but the illumination of the Holy Spirit in the power. All power is given to Jesus (Matt. 28:18 KJV). The Holy Spirit reveals Him—all power and fullness are through Him. The Holy Spirit conveys to the mind all the fullness in Him. The blood of Jesus purifies the position of the believer. After the blood, he can be a perfect offering.

The Holy Spirit then takes the position of sanctifying the whole of our actions, but all is for the glory of the Son. The human is never in it. The human exists for the purpose of manifesting the glory of God—the channel never robbing the glory, the Spirit so sanctifying the act. We are to live all the time not conformed but transformed, raising the mind through the sanctifying of the will and desires— the sanctifying of every thought. In this way, we are robbed of all pride and exaltation. We are so sanctified by the Spirit that nothing hinders the manifestation of the glory of God, and we are included in the perfection of the will of God.

The epistles of the apostle Paul were all written to people baptized with the Holy Spirit. Here you touch deep water—the Holy Spirit must be in control so that you are able to read and to understand what God intends you to be. In Ephesians, we read, "According to the purpose of God and according to the will of God." (See Ephesians 1:11.) The simplicity of the truth, *"the sincere milk of the word"* (1 Pet. 2:2 KJV). Jesus said, *"Learn from Me, for I am gentle and lowly in heart*" (Matt. 11:29). And John wrote, "'*The anointing which you have received from Him abides in you*' (1 John 2:27) and will teach you all things." (See verse 27.)

Regarding the "*sanctification of the Spirit*" (1 Pet. 1:2), the Holy Spirit alone gives the utterance. After the cleansing by the blood comes the sanctification of the Spirit. You no longer have any human desire, but your mind is more and more purified for the glory of God. When we get into the Spirit, time has gone. In the Spirit and the glory, "*a thousand years* [are] *as one day*" (2 Pet. 3:8). If I live in the Spirit, I have no dreary days. Some days the sun shines more, but it makes no difference.

We are not in Egypt's sand. Oh, you must not look for me down in Egypt's sand. (See Acts 7:37–41.) The Holy Spirit wants to perfect in us what He has begun. It was God who sought and drew our hearts until we prayed in the Spirit. That is how we began and how we must continue. "*This is what was spoken by the prophet Joel*" (Acts 2:16); and if you think it out, "*this*" means God—God's work in us. God has been pouring out His Spirit, waking us up to a new order in the Spirit. The Spirit has begun to breathe through the land.

Something must be happening. We pay a big price for it—much weeping, travailing, and groaning—and we cannot get out of it. But God is going before us.

We need no questions—it is a poor people who cannot praise the Lord. Suppression of praise never disturbs the Devil. God wants firebrands, lives aflame by the power of God. God has made me so hungry. I was never so hungry and thirsty for God as I am now. We are at a place where it is not "It will be," but "It must be." If we will pay the price, God will open the heavens. I am doing all I know to meet the will and mind of God, so that God may bring us a deluge of the latter rain.

A perfect blending for God's glory is Jesus manifesting the glory of the Father, full of the Holy Spirit; the Holy Spirit revealing the Son, reflecting the Son, the King of Glory, to bring millions out of darkness into light, for the glory of the King of Glory.

And God will be revealed. God is bringing us to a place wholly separated unto Himself—sanctified in spirit, soul, and body (1 Thess. 5:23). Separated unto Him—going in and out and finding pasture (John 10:9), and able to feed the multitude with the Bread of Life. In this is abundance of peace. We are debtors to God, who has chosen us and brought us to a desired place, inspiring us. We never know how weak we are until we are covered by His mighty strength. Then we will not fail, but we will stand for God, *"and having done all,* [will] *stand"* (Eph. 6:13); Jesus will carry us through.

Surrender all with a fresh consecration. Let us be better saved now than when we began; let us have more knowledge of God—causing us to triumph in Him—more holiness, and deeper abasement.

Believe God. Give yourselves wholly to Jesus, with a large heart, a whole heart, perfectly yielding to God, God controlling every thought.

Oh, Lord, have me for Your glory! Have I obtained this? Yes! For he who asks, receives (Matt. 7:8). Now, don't fail God. Believe, and it will come to pass! Whatever you desire when you pray, God will grant it (John 15:7). This day, can God fill me with His Spirit? Yes, when I ask. *Will* He fill me? Yes! If I ask in faith.

Yes, filled with God,
Yes, filled with God;
Pardoned and cleansed,
And filled with God.

We come to an end of self and are filled with God. Stand with God for the new day. The self has been put out, and the curse has been put away from us. (See Galatians 3:10–13.) Filled with God, and Jesus glorified! Amen.

10

ORDINATION

God wants, by the power of the Spirit, to reveal to us our position in Christ. We see that Jesus foreshadowed blessings that were to come. Most of His ministry was a type of what the believer is to enter into. Let us see what God had in mind to do for us through His Son:

> You did not choose Me, but I chose you and appointed ["ordained," KJV] you that you should go and bear fruit, and that your fruit should remain, that whatever you ask the Father in My name He may give you.   (John 15:16)

Oh, to realize the fact of ordination! What will bring it—will we stand before God? He wants us to be right up-to-date in everything, and the Spirit of the Lord will be able to bring before our minds what the mind of the Spirit is concerning us, so that we may step into all the privileges.

God wants a strong people. Remember the charge God gave Joshua. First He said, "Be full of courage; be neither dismayed nor discouraged," and then He gave him the charge. (See Joshua 1:6–9; 8:1.) If God forecasts anything for you, He will give the power to carry it through. So, after God had given Joshua the word, He said, "Now it will depend upon your living day and night meditating upon the Word of God." (See Joshua 1:7–8.) As you come into this blessed state of holy reverence for the Word of God, it will build you up also, and make you strong.

"Then you will have good success" (v. 8). God told Joshua that, in this state of grace, whenever he put his foot forward, he was not to let it slide back but to have the other foot ready to go forward. The Devil brings back to people's minds things that they did so long ago, and there they are, thinking about them day and night! There are two things that are certain, and there is a third thing that is more valuable than either of the first two. One is that the Devil doesn't let you forget your sins; the second is that you never forget them; and the third is that God *has forgotten them.* The question is whether we are going to believe God, the Devil, or ourselves. God says that our sins are passed, cleansed, gone! You cannot go on with God until you stand on His Word as cleansed, with your heart made pure. Standing on this blessed Rock, you can step forward and make inroads into the Devil's camp, overthrow all his tactics, and bring desolation to his power as you realize that your sins are forgiven and finished with.

God has ordained us. But people allow Satan to say to them, "Yes, but that was only the disciples' order." I tell you, beloved, that God's order is for the church. What He said to the disciples, He says to us. If we can believe, God has ordained by the Holy Spirit to fill us and clothe us until we know we are the chosen of God, precious in His sight to carry the vessels of the Lord (Isa. 52:11); and we are not only to be coworkers with Him, but also to *"arise to [our] inheritance"* (Dan. 12:13), dividing the powers of Satan.

This salvation is too big and great for any mind to take in. It is only the flash of eternity, the divine light of heaven, the Spirit of the living God with His infinite mind that can flash into the caverns of the human soul until we see the whole heaven and are changed by His power so that there is not a weak point, not an unbelieving attitude, because the Word has so changed us that we are a perfect pattern of the new covenant of Christ.

The ordination can be finished, but there still may be a lack of power. The credentials are all right, but the power is not there. Jesus said, "I have ordained you; I have chosen you *'that you should go and bear fruit, and that your fruit should remain, that whatever you ask the Father in My name He may give you'* (John 15:16)." I believe that God wants us to know that our fruit has to remain. Beloved, we should recognize that our prayers are in vain unless we really expect what we ask to be granted to us. (See James 1:5–7.)

"The word which they heard did not profit them, not being mixed with faith in those who heard it" (Heb. 4:2); but may God give us the word of faith, and then you will know for a fact that there is a great change in you. Even the preacher himself will be changed as he reads and preaches the Word. The Word quickens the preacher, the hearer, and everybody. The Word gives life, and God wants there to be such life in you that you will be moved as it is preached. Oh, it is lovely to think that God can change things in a moment, and can heal in a moment. When God begins, who can hinder Him?

Sometimes a thing comes before me, and I realize that nothing but the Word of God can meet the need. I meet all classes of people—even people who have no faith—and I find that the Word of God quickens them, even those who have no knowledge of salvation.

You often notice billboards with advertisements that would make it appear as if the thing advertised could cure everything. Oh, the gospel of the Lord Jesus Christ *does* cure everything!

One day, in Toronto, at the close of a service I was holding, I saw one of the leaders rush out as though something had happened, and when I got home, I found he had brought a man to me who was in a very strange way. He was a man of fine physique and looked quite all right, but his nerves were shattered throughout, and he asked me if I could do anything for a man who had not slept properly for three years. He said, "I have a business, a beautiful ranch and home, and it is all going. My whole nervous system is just in an awful state, and unless something happens, I will lose everything." He stood in front of me and asked for help. I said, "Go home and sleep." He protested, but I insisted that, without further protest, he must obey my command and *go*. He went home, got into bed, fell asleep, and slept all night. In fact, he told me afterward that his wife had to wake him.

He came along to see me again and said, "I have slept all night; I am a new man. The whole situation is changed now. I want to ask you another question. Can you get my money back? My business back? Can you get my house put in order again?" I said, "Yes—everything. You will not lose a thing. You be at the meeting tonight." I knew this man was a perfect stranger to salvation; he knew nothing about it. That night, he was in the audience, and I preached—not to him, for God has a better plan than for me to preach to any one person in a meeting. If God speaks, the whole thing will be done. He finishes the work, and it is my purpose to speak only for God; I am not seeking what to say to you; I am not trying to think of stories to tell you. God is the operator of my mind, and I am telling you all that He tells me to tell you. I am responsible to Him for you and must be faithful to you.

I preached the Gospel, which is *"the power of God to salvation"* (Rom. 1:16), and as I preached, this man became very uneasy. As I continued to preach, he became more and more restless; it seemed as though he could not bear to sit in his seat, and as I gave the altar call, he came rushing forward for salvation and for healing. As he started to come, he fell, the shot from God had gone so deeply into him that he could not get away.

Oh, it is lovely. *"Men and brethren,"* the crowds at Pentecost asked Peter and the other apostles, *"what shall we do?"* (Acts 2:37). The Gospel must be mightier than something that just moves your brains. Unless it moves your hearts, it is no good. God must bring into your hearts a real longing for Himself. You cannot be saved by feelings or by emotions; you can only be saved by the Word of the Lord. Now, this man fell down on his way to the altar, and I said, "Nobody touch him! No one speak to him. Keep your hands off the man; God has him in hand." And, oh, God made a fine job of him, and if you go to Toronto today, you will find that man worshipping the Lord, a wonderful citizen. He is out of the clutches of Satan, and everything has been squared up. Oh, when God begins to move, everything is soon in order. *"Seek first the kingdom of God and His righteousness, and all these things shall be added to you"* (Matt. 6:33).

JESUS CAN MEET EVERY NEED

Let me read a passage to you from Luke 8:

And behold, there came a man named Jairus, and he was a ruler of the synagogue. And he fell down at Jesus' feet and begged Him to come to his house, for he had an only daughter about twelve years of age, and she was dying. (Luke 8:41–42)

I would like you to take note of this man, Jairus, and his wife. They have a daughter whose needs nothing can meet. They have heard quite a lot about Jesus, and I can imagine the woman saying to her husband, "There's only one thing left. If you could see Jesus, our daughter would live." My brother, my sister, I tell you this: If you see Jesus, you will live. *You will*; and you can see Him now. God can so reveal Him to your hearts that while you are hearing this message, you will be able to see Jesus. He is in the midst; the power of God is over us. No man can say after hearing this message, "No man showed me the way." The Holy Spirit will show you the way of salvation, and oh, it is a wonderful way.

Think about Jesus. Did you ever think about Him? Talk about love! There is no love like His! His love has never changed. He loved us *"while we were still sinners,"* and then He died for us (Rom. 5:8). Nobody is saved when they are good; they are always saved when they are bad. God has a way of revealing our hearts to us, and when we see ourselves as sinners, He applies the balm.

Is it possible for anybody to seek Jesus and not find Him? Is it? Jairus went to seek Jesus. It is not possible for you to seek Jesus without finding Him. Those who seek Him, find Him, just the same as this man did. Glory to God! There is nothing in the world as lovely as the knowledge that God reaches out, and that those who seek Him, find Him—and He finds them. Remember, there are always two seekers. The moment you begin, you will find that God begins. When the Prodigal began to turn toward home, his father turned toward him. (See Luke 15:11–24.) Praise the Lord!

And when [Jairus] saw Him, he fell at His feet and begged Him earnestly, saying, "My little daughter lies at the point of death. Come and lay Your hands on her, that she may be healed, and she will live." (Mark 5:22–23)

And Jesus said, "I will come." (See verse 24.)

Oh, I do wish I were like Jesus. When I think that we left behind us at Melbourne, Australia, over 100 who were invalid and helpless and could not come to the meetings, and that we had no time to go to them! Oh, how my heart aches for those in similar circumstances! Jesus said, "I will come." Yes, it is lovely! You never need to be afraid that He will not find you if you seek Him. I tell you, my dear ones, it is impossible for God to fail you. If you hear the Word of God, it will so stimulate you that you will know as sure as you live that God will bring you out of your condition. It is impossible to know the Word of God without knowing that He will meet you.

Now, we read that they were traveling along the road toward the house of Jairus—and there was a great crowd of people all around Jesus—and just then we read about a certain woman (Luke 8:43–48). Hers was a rather interesting case. There is a little bit of arithmetic here that I would like you to notice. The woman had had an issue of blood for twelve years, and when she began to be sick, she had money. The physicians took all her money and left her worse than they found her! Now, I believe that doctors ought to be paid when they cure their patients—and not before. You all might find yourselves in a similar situation and finish up just where this woman did, and so there ought to be a new kind of arrangement. I am not against doctors. They have a work that no one else in the world has to do. Apart from salvation, they have a great suffering world of trials and sickness and sorrow to help. The world is full of trouble, and they are in the midst of it, for "*in the world you will have tribulation*" (John 16:33). However, Jesus said, "*In Me you may have peace*" (v. 33). "In the world—tribulation; but in Me—peace!"

I can just imagine that some people had been saying to this woman, "Oh, if you had only been with us today! We have seen such wonderful things; we are sure you would have been healed. I thought about you." And as they told this woman all about what Jesus had done that day, she said, "Oh, if I were only able to touch His garment, I believe I would be whole also." Was it possible? This woman was worse than she had been twelve years before. Beloved, I tell you that it is impossible for a single soul to have an inward desire of seeing and meeting with Jesus, and not to see and feel and *know* Him.

God's Word is true: "Those who seek Me will find Me." (See Jeremiah 29:13.) This woman was so moved by these stories that, day by day, she longed to see Jesus; and, glory to God, the day came. There was a great cry; all the people were thronging and surrounding Him on all sides and were rushing out of their houses and saying, "Oh, there He is!" She pushed her way in and *touched Him,* and the touch did it. God wants reality in your hearts, bringing you into the same determination to *touch Jesus!*

Jesus knew that if He had left us with only this part of the story before He ascended on high, no one here in Adelaide, Australia, would have been satisfied that they could be healed unless they could physically touch Him in the way that this woman did. So He changed the order of it and turned around and said, *"Who touched Me?"* (Luke 8:45). And Peter said, "That's a nice thing to say. Why, all the people are leaning against you; everybody's leaning against you." "Yes," He said, "but somebody *touched* Me." (See verses 45–46.)

Oh, there's a difference! You may lean about all your lives, but one atom of faith will do it. Come out of yourselves. No longer have an imaginary faith—get a reality, *believe,* and God will do it! Going back to our story, Peter said, "What do You mean, Lord?" And He said, "Someone has touched Me!" And then the woman turned around and said, "Yes, it was I; but I am so different now.

The moment I touched You, I was made whole!" (See Mark 5:29, 33.) Ah! Jesus answered her, *"Your faith has made you well. Go in peace"* (v. 34). Notice, He did not say "Your touch has made you well" but "Your faith," and beloved, it is faith that will bring results now in your life.

Oh, blessed be God, it is a living faith. You say, "Tell me how to get it." You can have it for about six pounds. "What?" you ask. That's how much it costs to buy a Bible, the Word of God. *It is faith.* His Word is the authority of faith. It is the living principle of faith. *"If you can believe"* (Mark 9:23), Jesus said. Believe what? Believe what the Word says. The people came and asked Jesus, *"What shall we do, that we may work the works of God?"* (John 6:28). He said, *"This is the work of God, that you believe in Him whom* [God] *sent"* (v. 29, emphasis added). *"This is the work of God."* Oh, beloved, I would be a poor man without the Word of God, but I am rich:

My heavenly bank, my heavenly bank,

The house of God's treasure and store;

I have plenty up there—I'm a real millionaire,

And I will go poor no more.

Oh, the Word of God—the Living Word—the precious, precious, Word of God. Jesus said, *"You search the Scriptures, for in them you think you have eternal life; and these are they which testify of Me"* (John 5:39). Hallelujah!

"ONLY BELIEVE"

Continuing with our story, just when everyone was getting to see that Jesus was everything, into the midst of the throng the Devil came. Yes, he always comes at a busy time. Four or five people rushed from the house of Jairus, right into the presence of Jesus, and took hold of Jairus and said, "Look here! Don't trouble Jesus anymore; your daughter is dead. He can do nothing for a dead daughter." (See Mark 5:35.) But Jesus said, *"Only believe"* (v. 36). And may God help us to believe. Only to believe! Oh, what blessing it is if we believe. Allow God to divest you of everything else right now, beloved. Allow the Word to sink into your hearts. Allow it to drive away everything else. Eternal life is available for you who will believe.

Your faces are an inspiration as I look at you and see your eternal destiny. I see that God, the Holy Spirit, can make every person, without exception, *"heirs"* and *"joint heirs"* (Rom. 8:17) with Him. You can be saved by the power of the faith that I am speaking to you about. Only believe. You cannot save yourself. The more you try in your own strength, the more you get "fixed up"; but, oh, if you will believe, God will save you. He will do it. You will know that God saves. *"Bless the LORD, O my soul; and all that is within me, bless His holy name!"* (Ps. 103:1).

Sometimes our faith is tested. For twenty-five years, Abraham believed God. God had said to him, "Your wife will have a son." (See Genesis 17:15–16.) Every year, his wife grew weaker. He saw her wrinkles and her frail, weak condition. Did he look at it? No—he looked at the promise. For twenty-five years, God tested him; but he gave glory to God and considered neither Sarah's body nor his own, and as he did so, God said, "Yes, Abraham." Pay close attention to what the Word says:

> *And not being weak in faith, [Abraham] did not consider his own body, already dead (since he was about a hundred years old), and the deadness of Sarah's womb. He did not waver at the promise of God through unbelief, but was strengthened in faith, giving glory to God, and being fully convinced that what He had*

promised He was also able to perform. And therefore "it was accounted to him for righteousness." Now it was not written for his sake alone that it was imputed to him, but also for us. It shall be imputed to us who believe in Him who raised up Jesus our Lord from the dead, who was delivered up because of our offenses, and was raised because of our justification.

(Rom. 4:19–25)

All who believe *"are blessed with faithful Abraham"* (Gal. 3:9 KJV), and God wants to show us that nothing is impossible to those who believe (Mark 9:23).

I would like God to reveal Himself to us all. People say to me, "How long will it be before I am healed?" And I ask, "How long will it be before you believe God?" I would like you to imagine the ten lepers that Jesus healed. Look at them for a moment. You never saw such a group in your life. Some were blind; some were lame and maimed; and there they were, all wanting to get to Jesus! They saw Him and shouted to Him, for they were not allowed to go near others. They shouted and said, *"Jesus, Master, have mercy on us!"* (Luke 17:13). And He shouted and answered them in this way: *"Go, show yourselves to the priests"* (v. 14). Was it an impossibility? Yes, humanly speaking. But the lame lepers were helped by the other lepers who were not lame, and the blind by those who could see, and the whole group went their way, and *"as they went,"* they were healed (v. 14). As they believed, they were healed. Hallelujah! And one said, "I'm not going any farther; I'm not going to see the priest; I'm going back to see the man who healed us." So he turned back and said to Jesus, "I'm one of the ten." "Well," said Jesus, "where are the other nine? Are you the only one who came to give God glory?" (See verses 15–19.) That is the way with people today. They get saved and healed, and they don't tell it out for the glory of God. Why is it that people don't tell what God has done for them?

> The Lord told His disciples to proclaim
>   everywhere
> The gospel of redemption to hearts
>   o'erwhelmed with care;
> "But tarry at Jerusalem till pow'r from
>   heaven descend,
> And lo, will I be with you, even till the
>   world doth end."
>
> These signs shall follow them that believe
>   upon My name—
> Go, preach ye the Gospel, then will I confirm
>   the same.

11

POSSESSION OF THE REST

I believe that it is in the perfect will of God that I read to you the entire fourth chapter of the book of Hebrews. We have here one of those divine truths that is so forceful in all of its bearings to us.

> *Therefore, since a promise remains of entering His rest, let us fear lest any of you seem to have come short of it. For indeed the gospel was preached to us as well as to them; but the word which they heard did not profit them, not being mixed with faith in those who heard it. For we who have believed do enter that rest, as He has said: "So I swore in My wrath, 'They shall not enter My rest,'" although the works were finished from the foundation of the world. For He has spoken in a certain place of the seventh day in this way: "And God rested on the seventh day from all His works"; and again in this place: "They shall not enter My rest." Since therefore it remains that some must enter it, and those to whom it was first preached did not enter because of disobedience, again He designates a certain day, saying in David,*

"Today," after such a long time, as it has been said: "Today, if you will hear His voice, do not harden your hearts." For if Joshua had given them rest, then He would not afterward have spoken of another day. There remains therefore a rest for the people of God. For he who has entered His rest has himself also ceased from his works as God did from His. Let us therefore be diligent to enter that rest, lest anyone fall according to the same example of disobedience. For the word of God is living and powerful, and sharper than any two-edged sword, piercing even to the division of soul and spirit, and of joints and marrow, and is a discerner of the thoughts and intents of the heart. And there is no creature hidden from His sight, but all things are naked and open to the eyes of Him to whom we must give account. Seeing then that we have a great High Priest who has passed through the heavens, Jesus the Son of God, let us hold fast our confession. For we do not have a High Priest who cannot sympathize with our weaknesses, but was in all points tempted as we are, yet without sin. Let us therefore come boldly to the throne of grace, that we may obtain mercy and find grace to help in time of need.

(Hebrews 4)

God wants us all to see that we must not come short of that blessed rest that is spoken of to us in this passage. I am not speaking about the rest there is through being saved, although that is a very blessed rest. I am not speaking about the rest we have in the body when pains have gone away, or of the rest that comes because of not having sin, when sanctification has worked in a wonderful way by the blood of Jesus. Rather, God wants me to speak about the rest in which you cease from your own works (Heb. 4:10), and where the Holy Spirit begins to work in you, and where you know that you are not your own, but are absolutely possessed by God.

Beloved, I ask you to diligently follow me along these lines, because there are so many people who are not at rest; they have no rest—they are unrestful in so many ways. I believe that God can bring us into places of rest this day where we will cease from our own works, where we will cease from our own planning, where we will cease from our own human efforts, from our self-assertiveness, which so interfere with God's power within us. God wants to fill our entire beings with Himself, yes, to fill us so full of Himself that "we" are not. For God will take us into His plan, His pavilion, His wisdom, *"and the government will be upon His shoulder"* (Isa. 9:6). Remember that wonderful word that Jesus said to Peter:

When you were younger, you girded yourself and walked where you wished; but when you are old, you will stretch out your hands, and another will gird you and carry you where you do not wish. (John 21:18)

In the twentieth chapter of Acts, Paul said, *"I go bound in the spirit"* (v. 22); all that had to be done was not done by him, because the Holy Spirit was doing it. I want to take you for a moment into Acts 15 and 16 where, in the power of the Holy Spirit—remember, it was only in the power of the Holy Spirit—Paul, Silas, Barnabas, Mark, John, and Peter learned a great plan in their lives. That plan was that there had to be Another mightier than they, holding them, choosing for them, even their words, their thoughts. For their lives had to be so divinely in the Holy Spirit that they would know exactly -what to do, and do it at the right time. (See Acts 15, especially verse 28, and Acts 16:1–10.)

Let us turn for only a moment to a wonderful chapter, the sixteenth chapter of Acts, so that we may have some idea as to what it means to have the Holy Spirit leading us all the time. I call your attention to the sixth verse: "*Now when they had gone through Phrygia and the region of Galatia, they were forbidden by the Holy Spirit to preach the word in Asia.*"

Now, you might say, "Did not Asia have as much need for the Holy Spirit as anywhere else?" Certainly! Exactly so, but the Holy Spirit knows who is ready to receive the Holy Spirit. There may be a need, but the people may not be ready. You may need lots of things, but if you are not ready for them, you will not get them. What does it mean to be ready and needy? It means to be ready and *hungry*, to be so hungry that you cannot rest unless you get everything God has for you. God can bring you there.

> *After they had come to Mysia, they tried to go into Bithynia, but the Spirit did not permit them. So passing by Mysia, they came down to Troas. And a vision appeared to Paul in the night. A man of Macedonia stood and pleaded with him, saying, "Come over to Macedonia and help us."* (Acts 16:7–9)

Ah, that was the place where they needed help, that was the place where there was a cry for God. You need, beloved, to pray through so that this city of Wellington, New Zealand, requires help; then she will get the blessing. Beloved, there is such a thing as people thinking that they are full and rich, and not knowing that they are hungry, poor, and blind. (See Revelation 3:17.) The worst thing that can come to anyone, to a child of God, is to be self-satisfied with his present spiritual attainment—it is an awful position. Oh, what a startling truth we have in Revelation 3:15: "*I know your works, that you are neither cold nor hot. I could wish you were cold or hot.*"

Beloved, I want to preach to you by the grace of God in order to move you so that you cannot rest until God so gets you for Himself that you will become bread for the people, water for the thirsty ground. There is no one, either young or old, whom God cannot meet. God has grace for us all. God does not want anyone to be lukewarm. God is looking for a hungry people, a thirsty land.

Then, beloved, I notice that many people here fall short of coming into line with this divine blessing because of unbelief. The last time I was in Wellington, I met people who had been Christians and who had been breaking bread for years, but who were filled with unbelief; they will not accept the right way of the Lord. They break bread, but they won't tow the line. May God save us from such a position. Now, this is unbelief, and nothing else; but when the Holy Spirit comes, then unbelief is moved away and people are humble, brokenhearted, thirsty; they want God. May God keep us humble and hungry for the Living Bread. God is showing me that you cannot have this blessed power upon you unless you become hungry.

Now, we have in the Scriptures some very clear truths that are so full of life and power that you never need to be ashamed of the Gospel; it is so full of life and power. May God give us grace to enter in.

CEASING FROM OUR OWN WORKS

I want you to notice that the Word of God is so clear. If you turn to the Scriptures, you will find that the whole history of the nation of Israel is a plan for us to see that God would have taken them on to many victories, but He could not because of their unbelief. They were eligible for all the fullness of God; however, not a single one of the original Israelites who had been freed from Egypt entered into the Promised Land except Joshua and Caleb. The reason they went in was because they had *"a different spirit"* (Num. 14:24). Have you never read about this? Joshua and Caleb had a different spirit.

The Spirit was so mighty upon Joshua and Caleb that they had no fear; the Holy Spirit upon them had such a dignity of reverence for God that these two people brought the bunches of grapes and presented them before the people. (See Numbers 13:17–14:9.) Ten other people were sent out, but they had not received the Spirit, and they came back murmuring. If you get filled with the Spirit, you will never murmur anymore. I am speaking about the people who get the Holy Spirit and go on—not the people who remain stationary, but those who go straight forward.

When these other ten people came back, they were murmuring. What was wrong? They had no rest. "*There remains therefore a rest for the people of God. For he who has entered His rest has himself also ceased from his works*" (Heb. 4:9–10), and then God begins to work. These ten people and the rest of the Israelites said, "We will become prey to the people of the land, and our children will be slain by them." So God said to them through Moses, "Your children will go in, and you will be shut out." (See Numbers 14:2–3, 27–35.) It was unbelief alone.

I pray to God the Holy Spirit that you will search your hearts, and the Word, and see if you have received this Spirit. What is this Spirit? The Holy Spirit. To have received is to be filled with the Holy Spirit, filled with the life of the Spirit, what we call unction, revelation, force. What do I mean by force? Force is that position in the power of the Spirit where, instead of wavering, you go through, and instead of judgment, you receive truth. May God help us.

THE HOLY SPIRIT MANIFESTS THE WORD IN THE BODY

I want to give you a very important point about the Holy Spirit. The Holy Spirit is the only power that manifests the Word in the body.

For the word of God is living and powerful, and sharper than any two-edged sword, piercing even to the division of soul and spirit, and of joints and marrow, and is a discerner of the thoughts and intents of the heart. (Heb. 4:12)

Investigate what I have said, and when I give you a chance to ask questions bearing on the Word, God will be able to help me to help you to rest concerning these deep truths. Let us read that verse again, along with verse thirteen:

For the word of God is living and powerful, and sharper than any two-edged sword, piercing even to the division of soul and spirit, and of joints and marrow, and is a discerner of the thoughts and intents of the heart. And there is no creature hidden from His sight, but all things are naked and open to the eyes of Him to whom we must give account.

I want to deal now with the breath of the Spirit on the Word of God, which will give you rest. There is not a person who understands, or gets into revelation, on this Word who would be deaf; there is not a person who would suffer indigestion, not a person who would have rheumatism. There is no such thing as any evil power being in you if you understand this Word. I want to give it to you so that you may understand it.

Concerning the breath of the Holy Spirit, we have, in the second chapter of Acts, one of the most divine fundamental revelations. When the Holy Spirit came like a *"rushing mighty wind"* (Acts 2:2) and filled the place where the disciples were, divided tongues of fire sat upon each of them, and they were filled with—what? Wind? Breath? Power? A Person? They were filled with God, the third person of the Trinity. The Holy Spirit filled their bodies.

I can declare to you that not one of the 120 disciples at Pentecost had the slightest defect in their bodies when they came out of the house in which they had gathered. I have seen people filled with the Holy Spirit who used to be absolutely helpless, and when the power of God took their bodies, they became like young men instead of old, withered people. This is the power of the Holy Spirit. But now I am going to show you the reason.

"*The Word of God is living and powerful*" (Heb. 4:12). Paul said, "*You He made alive*" (Eph. 2:1). The Word of God is powerful for pulling down the strongholds of Satan. I would like you to read 2 Corinthians 10:4–5:

> *For the weapons of our warfare are not carnal but mighty in God for pulling down strongholds, casting down arguments and every high thing that exalts itself against the knowledge of God, bringing every thought into captivity to the obedience of Christ.*

Now, the Holy Spirit will take the Word, making it powerful in you until every evil thing that presents itself against the obedience and fullness of Christ will absolutely wither away. I want to show you the need of the baptism of the Holy Spirit, by which you know that there is such a thing as perfect rest, a perfect Sabbath, coming to your life when you are filled with the Holy Spirit; and I want you to see perfect rest in this place. I want you to picture Jesus on earth, filled with the Holy Spirit. On one occasion, He—filled with the Holy Spirit—lay asleep on a boat, and a storm began so terribly and filled the ship with water, until His disciples cried out, "*Lord, save us! We are perishing!*" (Matt. 8:25). He rose (filled with the Holy Spirit, remember) and rebuked the wind. He asked, "*Why are you fearful?*" (v. 26).

I want you to see, beloved, that when the Holy Spirit comes into your life, even if your house were to catch on fire, you would be at rest. The Lord protects His own.

Come a little nearer. I want you to see that this Holy Spirit, this divine Person, has to get so deep into us that He can destroy every evil thing. *"Living and powerful, and sharper than any two-edged sword, piercing even to the division of soul and spirit, and of joints and marrow"* (Heb. 4:12).

Some people, after being saved, get pain in their lives because of soulishness. Any number of saved people are soulish, as described in Romans 7. They want to do good, but they find evil, and they continue to do the thing they hate to do (v. 19). What is going on? They need the baptism of the Holy Spirit. Why? The baptism of the Holy Spirit is necessary, for then the Holy Spirit will so reveal the Word in the body that it will be like a sword; it will cut between the soul and the spirit; it will cut it right out until the soulishness cannot long to indulge in things contrary to the mind of God and the will of God anymore. Don't you want rest? How long are you going to wait before you enter into that rest? *"There remains therefore a rest for the people of God"* (Heb. 4:9). God wants you to enter into that rest:

> *For he who has entered His rest has himself also ceased from his works as God did from His. Let us therefore be diligent to enter that rest, lest anyone fall according to the same example of disobedience* ["unbelief," KJV].   (Heb. 4:10–11)

Enter into rest, get filled with the Holy Spirit, and unbelief will depart. Where people entered in, they were safe from unbelief, and unbelief is sin. It is the greatest sin, because it hinders you from all blessings.

THE WORD OF LIFE IN THE MARROW

There is a word that would be helpful to us, and I want you to take notice of it because it is so important. Let me read Hebrews 4:12 again:

For the word of God is living and powerful, and sharper than any two-edged sword, piercing even to the division of soul and spirit, and of joints and marrow, and is a discerner of the thoughts and intents of the heart.

I can move my elbow, my knee, and my shoulder, but these could not work properly if the marrow were to become congested. Now, hear about this salvation: God says that this Holy Spirit power will make the Word, this Christ of God, move in your marrow until there is not a stiff joint within you.

How we need the Holy Spirit! Now, probably, when you go outside, you will say, "He preached more about the Holy Spirit than anything." It is not so. My heart is so full of this theme—that Jesus is the Word—and it takes the Holy Spirit to make the Word act. Jesus is the Word that is mighty by the power of the Spirit for the pulling down of strongholds (2 Cor. 10:4), moving upon us so mightily that the power of God is upon us.

INTERPRETATION OF TONGUES

God has designed the fullness of the Gospel in its perfection and entirety, that where the breath of heaven breathes upon it, the Gospel, which is "the power of God unto salvation," makes everything form in perfect union with divine Trinity power until the whole man becomes a lively hope, filled with life, with fidelity, filled with God.

Remember that Jesus is Trinity; remember that Jesus is all fullness; remember that Jesus is the fullness of the Godhead (Col. 2:9); and the Holy Spirit makes Him so precious that—

It's all right now,

It's all right now,

For Jesus is my Savior,

And it's all right now.

I don't want it to be like when the unbelieving Israelites brought back the grapes from the Promised Land; they did not have the spirit that Joshua and Caleb had. I want you all to have a share. Oh, for the Holy Spirit to come with freshness upon us! Then you could all sing, "It's all right now." If it is not, it may be. God intends that it should be, and we are preaching in faith to you so that it *will* be.

It's all right now,

It's all right now,

For Jesus is *my* Savior,

And it's all right now.

Let me encourage you. God is a God of encouragement.

CLOTHED WITH CHRIST

Now I want to take you to the thirteenth verse:

There is no creature hidden from His sight, but all things are naked and open to the eyes of Him to whom we must give account. (Heb. 4:13)

"*No creature* [is] *hidden from His sight*"; all are naked before Him. Now, when God speaks of nakedness, He does not mean that He looks at flesh without clothing. God said, "*That you may be clothed, that the shame of your nakedness may not be revealed*" (Rev. 3:18). The nakedness referred to in this verse does not mean bodily but spiritual nakedness; but when Christ clothes you within, you have no spot (Eph. 5:27). He looks at your nakedness, at your weaknesses, at your sorrow of heart. He is looking into you right now, and what does He see?

HOLDING FAST OUR PROFESSION

Seeing then that we have a great high priest, that is passed into the heavens, Jesus the Son of God, let us hold fast our profession.   (Heb. 4:14 KJV)

What is our profession? I have heard so many people testifying about their profession. They have said: "Thank God, I am healed"; "Thank God, He has saved me"; "Thank God, He has cleansed me"; "Thank God, He has baptized me with the Holy Spirit." That is my profession—is it yours? That is the profession of the Bible, and God wants to make it your profession. You have to have a *whole* Christ, a *full* redemption; you have to be filled with the Holy Spirit, to be a channel for Him to flow through. Oh, the glorious liberty of the gospel of God's power.

Heaven has begun with me;

I am happy, now, and free,

Since the Comforter has come,

Since the Comforter has come.

BEING ALWAYS IN THE SPIRIT

It's all there. I know that God has designed this fullness, this rest, this perfect rest. I know He has designed it, and there should not be a wrinkle, a spot, a blemish (Eph. 5:27). The Word of God says, "Blameless and faultless." (See Philippians 2:15.) Praise the Lord for such a wonderful, glorious, inheritance, *through Him who loved us*" (Rom. 8:37). Hallelujah.

Beloved, you must come in, every one of you. This message is for the purpose of opening the door of your heart for God to move in until, if you were to go away and live in some solitary place, you would be full there the same as in this Wellington assembly; it would make no difference.

I think of the apostle John, as the legend goes, how they tried to destroy him by boiling him in oil, and tried other things to destroy him, and how he was exiled to the Isle of Patmos. He was in the Spirit there—he was on the island in the Spirit. Yes. It is possible to be in the Spirit while you are doing the wash, to be in the Spirit while you are scrubbing floors, to be in the Spirit under all circumstances.

Nothing really matters if the Lord loves me,

And He does, He does;

For nothing really matters if the Lord loves me,

And He does, He does.

For we do not have a High Priest who cannot sympathize with our weaknesses, but was in all points tempted as we are, yet without sin.   (Heb. 4:15)

There He is; there is the pattern; there is the Lord. You say, "Tell me something very wonderful about Him." Yes, I will tell you this: He loved us to the end (John 13:1); He had faith in us right to the end. Jesus never let go of the confidence that every soul would come right into the full tidemark. There it is for us today.

"*There remains therefore a rest for the people of God*" (Heb. 4:9). Some people say, "Oh, yes, it is a rest up there in heaven." No, no, no. That is not what I am talking about. This is a rest where we cease from our works (v. 10)—there are no works up there—where we cease from our own works, this day. I came to this meeting entirely shut in with God, and if God ever spoke in a meeting, He has spoken this morning. I may have been straight and plain about some things, but I had such a disturbing impression of Wellington when I was here the last time. I saw clearly that people were resisting the Holy Spirit, as much as when Stephen said, "*You stiffnecked and uncircumcised in heart and ears! You always resist the Holy Spirit; as your fathers did, so do you*" (Acts 7:51). Resisting the Holy Spirit.

Oh, if you won't resist the Holy Spirit, the power of God will melt you down; the Holy Spirit will so take charge of you that you will be filled to the uttermost with the overflowing of His grace.

12

GREATER, GREATER, GREATER

Praise the Lord! Well, if I could say all that my heart would like to say, I am sure this meeting would never come to an end. What a joy it is for the Lord to bring us together in this way, where we hear the words that are so precious and convincing of all that Jesus said. For there was never one who came to the world with such a loving compassion and who entered into all the needs of the people as Jesus did.

Now we see Jesus at the right hand of the Father (Mark 16:19), interceding with God for the needs of the people (Heb. 7:25), and there is something about His last message to the world that is so wonderful. Because He went to the Father, the Father cooperates with Him for the redemption of the world; and as a result of this, the Father will grant us all that we need. Jesus said, "If I go to the Father, I will send the Comforter." (See John 16:7 KJV.) He kept His word, and the Father kept His word, and that promise was made real on the Day of Pentecost.

He had ascended with the purpose of giving new power, new blessing, new vision, and a living faith to all those who would follow, so that the great work could be carried on. We have today, and for many days, been drinking at this measureless measure, which makes our hearts overflow with such rapture and delight, and we know we are living and moving in the power of the Holy Spirit! What wonderful things are held out to us. Now the vision is clear.

Many of you know how, as long back as twelve or fourteen years ago, we used to gather with small groups of people. Divine healing was a small thing in those days, but as we lived and moved among the people, they were healed, and they are healed today. God intended to work out His purpose, that we should loose people who are bound with graveclothes, and that they should be set free by the power of God.

We should be so filled with the power of God that we should not know what it is to have a body— that is, we should not be aware of our bodies through experiencing pain or sickness in them. Hallelujah! What I mean is this: all over the world, I tell people that ever since the Lord healed me over thirty years ago, I don't know what it is to have a body. Hallelujah! It is redemption in all its fullness not to have neuralgia, stomach trouble, kidney disease, indigestion, or rheumatism. Hallelujah! No lumbago, no corns— absolutely and entirely a new order of things. This is the inheritance of all who seek Him; this is the inheritance that there is in Jesus.

Jesus said to the Syro-Phoenician woman who asked Him to cast a demon out of her daughter, *"Let the children be filled first, for it is not good to take the children's bread and throw it to the little dogs"* (Mark 7:27). She answered in faith, *"Yes, Lord, yet even the little dogs under the table eat from the children's crumbs"* (v. 28). And Jesus, seeing her faith, replied, *"For this saying go your way; the demon has gone out of your daughter"* (v. 29). Hallelujah! There is bread, there is life, there is perfect healing from the Son of God. There is power in Him that removes every evil thing. It changes our circumstances and makes us know that the new creation is a living, vital thing. My word to you today is a special word because it is the word of the Master.

Jesus is moved with compassion as He sees us here today. Many people are around us who want a new vision of Jesus so that they may go away from this conference to carry on the work, for we are here to make disciples of the Nazarene. It is His will that we should do the works that He declared we would do.

There are two things in faith. There is a faith that acts, and there is a faith that needs to be accompanied by works, and we believe today that Jesus meant all that He said. Now let us look at what He said. It is found in three very important verses, and I trust that you will not forget them, whatever else you forget. What is the word? It is John 14:12–14:

> *Most assuredly, I say to you, he who believes in Me, the works that I do he will do also; and greater works than these he will do, because I go to My Father. And whatever you ask in My name, that I will do, that the Father may be glorified in the Son. If you ask anything in My name, I will do it.*

Looking at these verses, we are filled with joy. How I love, how I cherish, the words of Jesus; truly, they are lovely. When I think of the infinite wisdom of God in this measure, why did God not come to us and make Himself openly manifested to us? Why not? Because our finite beings could not stand His glory. You remember that as Saul went into Damascus, the light of the Son flashed brilliantly on the road, and those with him fell to the earth, and he was struck blind at the same time. We could not stand God's glory, because we are only finite beings, but God did the very best for us. When He could not present Himself to us, He gave us His Word.

His Word has a life-giving power. The psalmist knew it; he said that God's Word had given him life (Ps. 119:50). This Word is the divine revelation; it is the Word of life, of healing, of power. God has given us His own Word. I wish that all who can hear me would give themselves over to carefully reading more of the Word of God. If you only knew how I love it. There is something about the Word that is so wonderful. It brings new life into you until you realize you are a new creature. Hallelujah!

GOD IS GREATER THAN ALL

Let us look again at John 14:12:

Most assuredly, I say to you, he who believes in Me, the works that I do he will do also; and greater works than these he will do, because I go to My Father.

Oh, glory to God! God says, "Not one word will fail of all that I have promised." (See 1 Kings 8:56.) Sometimes we fail, but God never does. Hallelujah! What do I mean? Well, I am here today to get you to a place of resting upon the Word of God. If I can get you there, you can say in faith, "It is done." If I can speak to you today by the grace of God, it can be accomplished while you are sitting in your seat. The Word of God cannot fail, because it is the living Word. Listen to the words of Jesus as He says, "*Greater works than these* [you] *will do.*" I know as truly as I stand upon this platform that we will see the rising tide of blessing and divine healing go forth with greater power. But Satan will always try to hinder the real work of God. Whenever the power of God is being manifested, Satan will be there trying to upset it.

Satanic forces will be there, but God is greater. When we were baptized in the Holy Spirit, the Spiritualists learned of it and came to one of our meetings. They heard that we were speaking in tongues, and they came and filled two rows. Then I began speaking in tongues (that was natural to me), and then these muttering devils began also. I went to these two rows and I said, "Go out, you devils, go out," and they went out like a flock of sheep! They went right outside, and when they got outside, they cursed and cursed, but they were outside. So I know that the Devil will have manifestations, but in the name of Jesus, his power is gone.

What I want to impress upon you is that we must see these greater works that the Lord promised we would see. Let us hear the words of our Lord again: *"Greater works than these [you] will do, because I go to My Father. And whatever you ask in My name, that I will do, that the Father may be glorified in the Son"* (John 14:12–13). What is it that you want? *"Whatever you ask in My name, that I will do."* Glory to God. Is there any purpose in it? Yes, *"that the Father may be glorified in the Son."*

If you want God to be glorified in the Son, if you want God to be glorified in Jesus, you must live in the position where these things are being done. Praise God, He has been delivering people in these meetings. Now, you people who have been delivered this morning, put up your hands. The power of God is here to deliver the people, but I am not satisfied. You think that I am satisfied? I have never seen anything yet to satisfy me. I am the hungriest person in this place!

GREATER POWER

There is something very remarkable and forceful in this verse: *"Most assuredly, I say to you, greater works than these* [you] *will do."* In the power of His name there is power against the Devil and all his hosts. It is a marvelous force against all these things. Glory to God. I will give you an illustration of this. In the course of my travels, I went to Sweden. While I was going along one day, I saw a man fall down in a doorway. People came along and said he was dead. I could not speak Swedish, but I could speak English, and the Devil knew I could speak English (he knows all languages). I used the power and authority of the name of Jesus, and instantly the man was delivered. The man had been troubled like this for years. The Lord told me to make him a public example, so I got him to come to the meeting, and he came and told us of his deliverance. He told us the most awful things that the Devil had been telling him, and then he told us how the Devil had gone right out of him. Praise God.

While I was in Ceylon, I was sent for to go to a certain place to pray for someone. I said, "What is the case?" It was a woman dying of cancer. I said, "Take this handkerchief in the name of the Lord." (See Acts 19:11–12.) But nothing happened. They said to me, "You must go this time." I went and looked at the woman. She was in a terrible condition, with cancer in the womb; she was nearly dead. The house was full of people, and I preached Jesus to them, and how precious He became to me as I did so. I said to them, "I know this woman will be healed, but I want you to know the power of my Lord. This case can be delivered, but I want you to know Him who can deliver." Jesus said, *"Greater works"*; what did He mean? Standing on the authority of the Word of God. Hallelujah!

The deliverance of this woman was so marvelous, and had such an effect on the family, that they went to the newspapers themselves and published it. The woman herself came to the meeting and stood up and told the people what great things the Lord had done for her. Hallelujah! *"Greater works than these [you] will do."* You say, "How?" Only believe. What is it to believe? It is to have such confidence in what the Lord said that we take Him at His word because He said it. Glory to God.

Yes, I know this Book is true,

Yes, I know this Book is true;

I'm acquainted with the Author,

And I know this Book is true.

WHATEVER YOU ASK

Let us look at the first part of this verse; it is very important: *"Whatever you ask in My name, that I will do, that the Father may be glorified in the Son"* (John 14:13). Tell me, what does *"whatever"* mean? It means everything. Redemption is so complete that the person who believes it is made complete. Our Master called the man who had the withered hand to stand before Him. (See Matthew 12:9–13.) Jesus looked at that withered hand, and at His command, the hand was restored. He gave the living word, *"Stretch out your hand"* (v. 11), and the hand was healed. People today are waiting for the *"revealing of the sons of God"* (Rom. 8:19). The world is crying out for something in accordance with the new creation order.

GOD IS ABLE TO DO EVERYTHING

I remember one day when a man came to see me about a woman who was dying, and he asked me to visit her. When we got to her room, I saw that there was no hope, as far as human aid was concerned. The woman was suffering from a tumor, and it had sapped her life away. I looked at her and I knew that there was no possibility of help except a divine possibility. Thank God, I knew He was able. I never say, "It cannot be." I find that God is able to do everything. I said to her, "I know you are beyond everything now, but if you cannot lift your arm, or raise it at all, it might be possible that you could raise your finger as an indication that you desire to get better." Her hand lay upon the bed, but she lifted her finger just a little. I said to my friend, "We will pray with her and anoint her." After we had anointed her, her chin dropped, death came on, and my friend said, "She is dead." He was scared; I have never seen a man so frightened in my life. He said, "What will I do?"

You may think that what I did was one of the most absurd things to do, but I did it. I reached over into the bed and pulled her out; then I carried her across the room and stood her against the wall and held her up, as she was absolutely dead. I looked into her face and said, "In the name of Jesus, I rebuke this death," and from the crown of her head to the soles of her feet, her whole body began to tremble. Then her feet stood on the floor, and I said, "In the name of Jesus, I command you to walk," and she began to walk. I repeated, "In the name of Jesus, in the name of Jesus, walk," and she walked back to the wardrobe, and then went back to bed.

My friend went out and told the people that he had seen a woman raised from the dead! One of the elders of the mission where she attended said that he was not going to have this kind of thing, and tried to stop it. The doctor heard of it and went to see the woman. He said, "I have heard from Mr. Fisher, the elder, that you have been brought back to life, and I want you to tell me if it is so." She told him it was so. He said, "Do you dare to come and give your testimony at a certain hall, if I take you in my car?" She said, "I will go anywhere to give it."

She came to the hall looking very white, but there was a lovely brightness on her face. She was dressed in white, and I thought how beautiful she looked. This is what she said: "For many months, I have been going down to death; now I want to live for my children. I came to the place where it seemed there was no hope. I remember a man came to pray with me, and he said to me, 'If you cannot speak or cannot lift your hands, if you want to live, move one of your fingers.' I remember moving my finger, but from that moment, I knew nothing else until I was in the glory. I feel that I must try and tell you what the glory is like. I saw countless numbers of people, and, oh, the joy and the singing, it was lovely! But the face of Jesus lit up everything, and just when I was having a beautiful time, the Lord suddenly pointed to me, without speaking, and I knew I had to go. The next moment, I heard a man say, 'Walk, walk, in the name of Jesus!' If the doctor is here, I would like to hear what he has to say."

The doctor rose. He had a white beard, and I cannot forget the color of his waistcoat; it was a canary-colored pattern. When he stood up, he began to speak, but he could not at first; his lips quivered and then his eyes looked like a fountain of waters. I thought, "Whatever is going to happen?" Then he said that for months he had been praying about the woman's condition, and at last he had felt that there was no more hope. He had told them at the house that the woman would not live much longer; in fact, it would only be a matter of days.

Not live? Hallelujah. But this is where the *"greater works"* come in.

Thank God, if we believe, all things are possible (Mark 9:23). It can be done now, this moment as you sit in your seat, if you believe it will be done for the glory of God. I ask you, while I preach, to believe God's Word, and it will come to pass. Glory to God. Now I want a wholesale healing today. I believe it may be possible for some to have that divine, inward moving of living faith that will make them absolutely whole. If you will deny yourself and believe God's Word, you will be healed at the touch of the Lord. Now I want you to live in the sunshine.

I went to Dover to preach, and twenty people were instantly healed at once. I have seen a hundred people instantly healed in a meeting, as they believed. People have been healed as they have risen from their seats. I want you to get to such a place of faith that you will not know you have a body. Mr. Stephen Jeffreys will be telling you tonight that there is a perfect redemption for all our needs. We want everyone in this meeting to go away with the knowledge of a full redemption. If you believe, on the authority of God's Word, that you are healed, you will have perfect health from the ends of your fingers to your whole body. We will sing this chorus,

I do believe, I will believe that Jesus

heals me now;

I do believe, I will believe that Jesus

heals me now.

13

OUR GREAT NEED: PAUL'S VISION

I want to speak of Pentecost and the fullness of the Spirit, and of what God is able to do with anyone who is yielded to Him. We are here today for one purpose, and that is to kindle one another with a holier zeal than has ever possessed us before. I believe there is a greater need for us today in the world than ever before. There is more of a broken spirit abroad in our land than there has been for a long time past, and no one can meet the need today but the person who is filled with God.

God has promised to fill us. You may be filled with the mighty power of God, and yet, in a way, you may not realize it; still, you may know that you are being used by a power apart from yourself, a power that keeps you from self-exhibition. Just as the sun by its mighty power brings certain resources to nature, I believe the power of God in the human soul, the power filling it with Himself, is capable, by living faith, of bringing about what otherwise could never be accomplished. May God by His Spirit prepare us for what He has to say.

A LIGHT FROM HEAVEN

I want to draw your attention to Acts 26:12–19, where we are told of the *"light from heaven"* (v. 13) and the voice that arrested Paul on his way to Damascus; where we are told of his conversion, and of the commission given to him to go to the Gentiles *"to turn them from darkness to light, and from the power of Satan to God"* (v. 18), and of the fact that he *"was not disobedient unto the heavenly vision"* (v. 19). Paul gave this account of his experience to King Agrippa:

> *As I journeyed to Damascus with authority and commission from the chief priests* [to arrest the Christians there], *at midday, O king, along the road I saw a light from heaven, brighter than the sun, shining around me and those who journeyed with me. And when we all had fallen to the ground, I heard a voice speaking to me and saying in the Hebrew language, "Saul, Saul, why are you persecuting Me? It is hard for you to kick against the goads." So I said, "Who are You, Lord?" And He said, "I am Jesus, whom you are persecuting. But rise and stand on your feet; for I have appeared to you for this purpose, to make you a minister and a witness both of the things which you have seen and of the things which I will yet reveal to you. I will deliver you from the Jewish people, as well as from the Gentiles, to whom I now send you, to open their eyes, in order to turn them from darkness to light, and from the power of Satan to God, that they may receive forgiveness of sins and an inheritance among those who are sanctified by faith in Me." Therefore, King Agrippa, I was not disobedient to the heavenly vision.* (Acts 26:12–19)

You remember how it is stated in Acts 9 that for three days after this vision, Paul was blind; he was in a state in which he could not see, in a state of brokenheartedness, I suppose. And then God had him.

It is a wonderful thing when God gets you. You are not much good for anything until God gets you. When God gets you, you are loose and you are bound: you are free, but you can act only as He wills for you to act; and when you act only for Him, there is in the process that which brings out something mighty for all time.

Well, Paul first had to come to this time of crying, weeping, contrition, heart-meltedness, yieldedness. He had done all he could in the natural, but the natural had only brought him to a broken place, to blindness, to helplessness, and this had to come out of Paul's life before he could have the life of God. When we have altogether parted with our own, as it were, then there is a possibility of God's likeness being made manifest in us, of the Water of Life filling us and not only fertilizing our own life, but also flowing from us as a river that will touch others. No one can tell what a river can do when it is set aflow by God, because when God is in the plan, everything works mightily and harmoniously. I pray to God the Holy Spirit that at all times I may cease from everything except the thing that God wants to bring out—not what I want to bring out.

There are so many wonderful things about a life filled with the Holy Spirit that one feels almost as if one could never stop speaking of them. There are so many opportunities and such great forces that can never come in any other way. When Jesus had come to a place where He would not make bread for Himself (see Matthew 4:3–4), I find that He reached a place where He could make bread for thousands (see Matthew 14:15–21; 15:32–38). And when I come to a place where I will not do anything for myself, then God will do something for me, and I will gladly do anything for Him that He may desire me to do. That is in the order of the baptism of the Spirit. It is when we cease to clothe ourselves that God clothes us; and it is the clothing with which He clothes us that covers all our nakedness.

In his helplessness and brokenness, Paul cried, "*Lord, what do You want me to do?*" (Acts 9:6). That cry reached to heaven, and, as a result, a holy man came, who was touched with the same fire and zeal that filled his Master, and he laid his hands upon Paul and said, "*Receive your sight and be filled with the Holy Spirit*" (Acts 9:17).

INTERPRETATION OF TONGUES

The living touch of the river of the life of God is what makes all things akin and brings a celestial glory into the human heart, and phrases that meet the kindled desire therein.

When God moves a man, his body becomes akin with celestial glory all the time, and the man says things as he is led by the Holy Spirit who fills him. When we are filled with the Holy Spirit, we go forth to see things accomplished that we could never see otherwise.

A VISION FROM GOD

First of all, Paul had a vision. There is always a vision in the baptism of the Spirit. But visions are no good to me unless I make them real, unless I claim them as they come, unless I make them my own; and if your whole desire is to carry out what the Spirit has revealed to you by a vision, it will surely come to pass. Lots of people lack the power because they do not keep the vision, because they do not allow the fire that has come to infuse them and to continue to burn. There must be a continuous burning on the altar. Holy Spirit power in a man is meant to be an increasing force, an enlargement.

God never has anything of a diminishing type. He is always going on. And I am going on. Are you going on? It is necessary, I tell you, to go on. You must not stop in the plains; there are far greater things for you on the hilltops than in the plains.

Jesus took particular care of Paul; He did not rush him through the business. Some people think that everything ought to be done in a tremendous hurry. With God, it is not so. God takes plenty of time, and He has a wonderful way of developing things as He goes along. Nothing that you undertake will fail if you do not forget what He has told you, and if you act upon it. You really cannot forget what the Holy Spirit brings right into your heart as His purpose for you. A man baptized by the Holy Spirit is no longer a natural man; he is forced by the Spirit; he is turned into another man. Joshua and Caleb could not say anything less than, "God, who has taken us and let us see the land, will surely give us the land." (See Numbers 14:6–9.)

Where are you fixed? Is God the Holy Spirit arranging things for you, or are you arranging things according to your own plan? A man filled with the Holy Spirit has ceased to be, in a sense; he has come to a rest; he has come to where God is working, to a place where he can *stand still, and see the salvation of the LORD*" (Exod. 14:13). What do I mean? I mean that such a man has *"ceased from his own works"* (Heb. 4:10 KJV) and abilities and associations. He will not trust his own heart; he relies only on the omnipotent power of the Most High; he is girded with Another. The man baptized with the Holy Spirit will always keep in touch with the Master in the passing crowd, or wherever he may be. He has no room for anything that steps lower than the unction that was on his Master, or for anything that hinders him from being about his Master's business.

If you are baptized by the Holy Spirit, you have no spiritual food apart from the Word of God, you have no resources but those that are heavenly. You have been *"planted"* with Christ (Rom. 6:5 KJV) and have been *"raised with Him"* (Col. 2:12), and you are seated with Him *"in the heavenly places"* (Eph. 2:6). Your language is a heavenly language; your source of inspiration is a heavenly touch; God is enthroned in your whole life, and you see things *"from above"* (James 3:17) and not from below.

A man who is baptized with the Holy Spirit has a Jesus mission. He knows his vocation, the plan of his life. God speaks to him so definitely and truly that there is no mistaking about it. Thank God for the knowledge that fixes me so solidly upon God's Word that I cannot be moved from it by any storm that may rage. The revelation of Jesus to my soul by the Holy Spirit brings me to a place where I am willing, if need be, to die for what the Word says.

The three Hebrew children, Shadrach, Meshach, and Abednego, said to King Nebuchadnezzar, *"We have no need to answer you in this matter"* (Dan. 3:16); and when a man of God is quickened by the Spirit, he never moves toward, or depends upon, natural resources. The furnace that is heated *"seven times more"* (v. 19) is of no consequence to the men who have heard the voice of God; the lions' den has no fearfulness for the man who opens his windows and talks to his Father. (See Daniel 6:5–10.) The people who live in the unction of the Spirit are taken out of the world in the sense that they are kept in the world without being defiled by the evil of the world.

A MINISTER AND A WITNESS

But let us come back to this wonderful vision that Paul had. I want you to see how carefully the Lord dealt with him:

But rise and stand on your feet; for I have appeared to you for
this purpose, to make you a minister and a witness both of the
things which you have seen and of the things which I will yet
reveal to you.   (Acts 26:16)

Do you not see how carefully the Lord works? He showed Paul
the vision as far as Paul could take it in, and then He said, "There
are other things that I will yet reveal to you." Did He ever appear to
Paul after that? Certainly, He did. But Paul never lost this vision; he
kept it up, so to speak. What was there in the vision that held him in
such close association with Jesus Christ that he was ready for every
activity to which he was led by the Holy Spirit? There were certain
things he had to do. Look, for instance, at Galatians 1:15–16. There
you will find a very wonderful word—a word that has had a great
impression upon me in relation to the subject of the continuation of
the baptism:

When it pleased God, who separated me from my mother's
womb and called me through His grace, to reveal His Son in
me, that I might preach Him among the Gentiles, I did not
immediately confer with flesh and blood.

Now read these words together: "*Therefore…I was not disobe-*
dient to the heavenly vision" (Acts 26:19) and "*I did not immediately*
confer with flesh and blood" (Gal. 1:16).

No one can be clothed in the Spirit and catch the fire and zeal
of the Master every day, and many times in the day, unless he ceases
in every way to be connected with the "*arm of flesh*" (2 Chron. 32:8)
that would draw him aside from the power of God. Many people
have lost the glory because they have been taken up with the natural. If we are going to accomplish in the Spirit the thing God has

purposed for us, we can never turn again to the flesh. If we are Spirit-filled, God has cut us short, brought us into relationship with Himself, and joined us to Another; and now He is *"all in all"* (1 Cor. 15:28) to us.

You may have a vision of the Lord all the time you are in a railway train, or in a streetcar, or walking down a street. It is possible to be lonely in the world and to be a Christian—unless what? Unless you cease to be a natural man. I mean that the Christian ought to have such an unction as to realize, at any moment, whether in the presence of others or alone, that he is with God. He can have a vision in the streetcar, or in the railway train, even if he has to stand with others in front of or behind him, or he can have a vision if he is there alone.

Nehemiah stood sadly before the king because of trouble in Jerusalem that had nearly broken his heart. He was sorrowful, and it affected his countenance; but he was so near to God that he could say, "I have communed with the God of heaven." (See Nehemiah 1:4–6.) And if we believers are to go forth and fulfill God's purpose for us, the Holy Spirit must be constantly filling us and moving upon us until our whole beings are on fire with the presence and power of God. That is the order of the baptism of the Holy Spirit. Then we are ready for every emergency.

Now, it is a most blessed thought—it struck me as I was reading at our assembly on Sunday morning—that in the holy, radiant glory of the vision that was filling Paul's soul, the people became so hungry for it that until midnight they drank at the fountain of his life. As he was pouring forth, a young man fell down from the third floor, and Paul, in the same glorious fashion as always, went down and embraced him and pressed the very life from himself into the young man, and brought him back to life. (See Acts 20:7–12.) There is always an equipping for emergency, a blessed, holy equipping by God!

Someone may call at your door and want to see you particularly, but you will not be able to be seen until you are through with God. Living in the Holy Spirit, walking in the divine likeness, having *"no confidence in the flesh"* (Phil. 3:3) but growing in the *"grace and knowledge"* of God (2 Pet. 3:18), and going on from one state of glorious perfection to another state of perfection—that is it. You cannot compare the Holy Spirit to anything less than, but to something more than, you ever thought about with all your thoughts. That is the reason why the Holy Spirit has to come into us to give us divine revelations for the moment. The person who is a "[partaker] *of the divine nature"* (2 Pet. 1:4) has come into a relationship where God imparts His divine mind for the comprehension of His love and for the fellowship of His Son. We are only powerful as we know that source; we are only strong as we behold the blessedness and all the wonderful things and graces of the Spirit.

HOLDING ON TO THE VISION

It was necessary for Jesus to live with His disciples for three years, to walk in and out among them, to manifest His glory, and to show it forth day by day. I will show you why it was necessary. Those men believed in God. But this Messiah, day by day, had to continually bring Himself into their vision, into their minds, into their very natures. He had to press Himself right into their lives to make them a success after He had ascended to heaven. He had to show them how wonderfully and gracefully and peacefully He could move the crowds.

And there were many crowds. You remember that the house to which they brought the paralytic man, and in which Jesus was speaking to the people, was so crowded that the paralytic's friends could not come near Him except by uncovering the roof and dropping the man through it. And Jesus healed the man. (See Mark 2:1–12.) Also, the way to the cities was so pressed with the people who were following Jesus and His disciples that He and they could hardly move along, but He always had time to stop and perform some good deed on the journey. (See, for example, Mark 5:22–34.)

What He had to bring home to the minds and hearts of the disciples was that He was truly the Son of God. They could never accomplish what they had to accomplish until He had proved that to them, and until He had soared to the glory. They could only manifest Him to others when He had imparted His life into the very core of their natures, making others confess that they were astonished, saying, *"We never saw anything like this!"* (Mark 2:12).

The Son of God traveled in the greatness of His strength to manifest before those disciples the keynote of truth that no one could deny. They had been with Him and seen His desire, His craving, His passion to serve God. Yes, He was passionate to be like God in the world, manifesting Him so that they might see what Philip had missed when he asked Jesus, *"Lord, show us the Father"* (John 14:8), and Jesus answered, *"Have I been with you so long, and yet you have not known Me, Philip? He who has seen Me has seen the Father; so how can you say, 'Show us the Father'?"* (v. 9). He wanted them to be clothed with the Spirit, baptized by the Spirit.

Some people get a wrong idea of the baptism. The baptism is nothing less than the third person of the blessed Trinity coming down from the glory, the Spirit of the triune God—who carries out the will of the Father and the Son—dwelling in your body, revealing the truth to you, and causing you sometimes to say "Ah!" until your heart yearns with compassion, as Jesus yearned, so that you travail as He travailed, mourn as He mourned, groan as He groaned. It cannot be otherwise with you. You cannot get this thing in a merely passive way. It does not come that way. But, glory to God, it does come. Oh, that God might bring from our hearts the cry for such a deluge of the Spirit that we could not get away until we were ready for Him to fulfill His purpose in us and for us.

I had a wonderful revelation of the power of God this past week. If there is anything I know about this baptism, it is this: it is such a force of conviction in my life that I am carried, as it were, through the very depths of it. Sometimes we have to think; at other times, we do not have time to think, and it is when we are at our wits' end that God comes and brings deliverance. When you are at your wits' end and you throw yourself on the omnipotent power of God, what a wonderful transformation there is in a moment.

I went to a house where they were very much distressed. It is a peculiar thing, but it is true, that the Spirit of the Lord upon a person either binds people together or makes them tremendously fidgety or restless so that they have to come to some place of decision. I know nothing like the mighty power of the Spirit; it works so harmoniously with the will of God. I was talking to the people in that house, and a young woman was there, and she said, "Oh, Father, I ought to have relief today. I am sitting here and I do know what to say, but somehow I feel that this whole trouble ought to go today." "What trouble?" I asked. "For six years, I have not been able to drink. I cannot drink. I go to the tea table and cannot drink. My body has gone down." I knew what it was. It was a devil in the throat.

You say, "You must be very careful about saying that." Well, I don't care who I offend by saying that; I believe that the Devil is the root of all evil, and it is a serious thing for a beautiful young woman who had perfect health, to otherwise be, as a result of that one thing, so disordered in her mind and body. I knew it was the power of Satan. How did I know? Because it attacked her at a vital point, and it got her mind on that point, and when it got her mind on that point, she went downhill, and she said, "I do not dare to drink; if I do, I will choke."

I asked the father and mother to go out of the room, and then I said to the young woman, "You will be free, and you will drink as much as you want, as soon as I am done with you, if you will believe. As surely as you are here, you will drink as much as you want."

Our brethren are going out into the streets tonight, and I may be among them, and they will be preaching, and they will say definitely, "Everyone who believes can be saved." They will mean, "Everyone who believes can be healed." It is the *same* truth. They will emphasize it over and over again. They have no more of a right to emphasize that than I have a right to say, *"He was wounded for our transgressions, He was bruised for our iniquities"* (Isa. 53:5).

So I said to her, "Now, do you dare to believe?" She said, "Yes, I believe that in the name of Jesus you can cast the evil power out." I then laid my hands upon her, and I said, "It's done; now, you drink." She went laughingly, praise God, and drew the first glass of water and drank. "Mother! Father! Brother!" she said, "I've drunk one glass!" There was joy in the house. What did it? It was the living *"faith of the Son of God"* (Gal. 2:20 KJV). Oh, if we only knew how rich we are, and how near we are to the fountain of life! *"All things are possible to him who believes"* (Mark 9:23).

When Aeneas, who had been bedridden for eight years, was told by Peter to *"arise and make your bed,"* and *"he arose immediately,"* (Acts 9:34), what did it? A life clothed with the Spirit.

INTERPRETATION OF TONGUES

The living water is falling and making manifest the Christ mission to those who will enter in by a living faith. Nothing can hinder the life-flow to those who believe, for "all things are possible to those who believe."

I wonder how many people have missed the point. If I talked to you for a short time, you would probably say to me, "I had a wonderful vision when I was baptized in the Spirit." I want you to notice that this vision that Jesus gave to Paul was right on the threshold of his baptism. An inspired life is always on the threshold of the quickening of that life by the Spirit. I want you to notice also that when a person is born of God, or when, as it were, God is born into the person and he becomes a quickened soul to carry out the convictions of the life of the Spirit of God in him—when he is born of God, instantly, on the threshold of this new birth, there comes a vision of what his life is to be. The question is whether you dare to go through with it, whether you are going to hold on to the very thing the Holy Spirit brought to you and never lose sight of it but press on in a life of devotion to God and of fellowship and unity with Him.

That is what Jesus did, that is what Paul did, and that is what we all have to do. In this connection, I want to say advisedly that when we are baptized with the gift of tongues, we must not allow tongues to entertain us, or be entertained by speaking in tongues. When you have accomplished one thing in the purpose of God for you, He intends for you to go forward and accomplish another. As soon as you accomplish one thing, it is, so to speak, no more to you, and God will enlarge you and equip you for the next thing He wants you to do.

When I was baptized in the Holy Spirit, a new era of my life unfolded, and I passed into that and rejoiced in the fact of it, and others with me. But the moment I reached that, God was ready with another ministry for me. If you are careful to watch for God, you will see that God is always caring for you. Jesus said, "If you honor Me here, I will honor you hereafter." (See John 12:26.) Whatever it may be that you are working out for God here, He is working out a far greater, a divine, glory for you. You have no need to be constantly talking about what you are going to appear like in the glory. The chief thing you are to be vigilant about is that you realize within yourself a deeper manifestation of the power of God today than yesterday, that you are clearer today regarding the mind of the Spirit than you were the day before, that nothing comes between you and God to cloud your mind. You are to see more of a vision of the glory of God today than yesterday, and to be living in such a state of bliss that it is heavenly to live. Paul lived in this ecstasy because he got into a place where the Holy Spirit could enlarge him more and more. I find that, if I continually keep my mind upon God, He unfolds things to me, and if I obediently walk before God and keep my heart pure and clean and holy and right, He will always be lifting me higher than I have ever expected to be.

LIVING SACRIFICES

How does this come about? Along these lines: In Romans 12:1, Paul spoke about a certain place being reached—he spoke about an altar on which he had laid himself. When he had experienced the mercies of the Lord, he could do nothing else than make a presentation of his body on the altar; it was always to be on the altar and never to be taken off. As soon as he got there, he was at the place where the Holy Spirit could bring out of him *things new and old* (Matt. 13:52), and, as we read in his epistles, *"things"* that Peter said were *"hard to understand"* (2 Pet. 3:16). How was that possible? Because he so lived in the Spirit that God brought His mind into Paul's mind, so that the apostle could write and speak, as an oracle of the Holy Spirit, things that had never been in print before, things portraying the mind of God. We read these things today and drink them in as a river, and we come out of the Epistles, as it were, clothed with mighty power, the power of God Himself.

How does this come about? It comes about when we are in a place that is low enough and where God can pour in, pour in, pour in. Paul could say that not one thing that God had spoken of him had failed. In Acts 26 and Romans 15, you will find that he accomplished all of what Jesus said he would accomplish, when he was reorganized, or filled, or infilled by the mighty power of God. God wants to do the same for you and for me, according to the gifts He has bestowed upon us. Will we stop short of what He says we ought to be; will we cease to come into line with the Mind that is always thinking for our best; will we cease to humble ourselves before Him who took the way of the Cross for us; will we withhold ourselves from Him who could weep over the doomed city of Jerusalem, from the Lord Jesus Christ, who has *"trodden the winepress alone"* (Isa. 63:3); will we cease to give Him our all? To what profit will it be if we hold back anything from Him who gives us a thousand times more than He ever asks from us? In Hebrews 2, He says He is going to bring *"many sons to glory"* (v. 10). It means that He is going to clothe them with His glory. Let that be your vision. If you have lost the vision, He is tender to those who cry to Him. He never turns away from the brokenhearted (Ps. 34:17–18), and those who seek Him with a whole heart will find Him (Deut. 4:29).

As I speak to you, I feel somehow that my heart is very much enlarged, that my compassion for my Lord is intensified, that nothing is too hard. The people in the days of the apostles took joyfully the confiscation of their goods (see Hebrews 10:34), and I feel there is a measure of grace given to the man who says, "I will go all the way with Jesus." What is that measure of grace? It is a clothing with hopefulness in pressing forward to the goal that God wants us to reach. But it is important that we do not forget the Lord Jesus' words, *"That no one may take your crown"* (Rev. 3:11). Paul saw there was a possibility that someone who had been the means of sowing the good seed of the Gospel might lose that for which God had taken hold of him (1 Cor. 9:27).

In closing, let me remind you that the Holy Spirit has brought us here. For what purpose has He brought us? Can anyone have come here, either seeker or speaker, without a cry to God to make some people today, as it were, flames of fire? My passion is that God will infuse you with such an anointing and cry that you won't be satisfied until you feel the very members of your body all on fire with a Spirit-kindled unity. It is not too late to put on the belt of truth today; it is not too late to put on the armor of God, to put on the shield of faith, to put on the sandals of the preparation of the gospel of peace better than ever before. (See Ephesians 6:13–17.)

God wants me to know and you to know that, experientially, we have only touched the very edge of this outpouring of the Spirit. If we do not allow God to fill us with Himself, He will choose somebody else. If we do not fall into line with the will of God, somebody else will. God is able to raise up people to carry out His commands. Jesus' disciples were glorifying Him one day, and the Pharisees told Jesus to rebuke them. "No," He said, "if these were to hold their peace, the very stones"—of which He could make bread—"would cry out." He could make them cry out. (See Luke 19:37–40.)

I have a Jesus like that, who can speak the word and the thing is done. I have a Jesus who indwells me and vitalizes me with a faith that believes it is true. I have a Jesus within me who has never let me get fainthearted or weary. Let us press on in faith according to God's will, and the outpouring that we have longed to see will come. Cheer up, hold on, never let go of the vision; be sure it is for you just as much as for anybody else, and God will surely make it come to pass. Never look down, because then you will only see the ground and miss the vision. All blessings come from above; therefore, keep your eyes on Jesus. Never weary. If you do not fall out along the way, He will be with you to strengthen you in the way. Hallelujah!

14

"THAT I MAY GAIN CHRIST"

I believe the Lord's will is that I read Philippians 3:1–14. It is the most blessed truth. God is revealing Himself in order to give us a vision of the Master. Paul had many visions of the Master, but there were many things that he had to be told because he was not among the disciples who walked with the Master when He lived on earth, nor was he connected with those plans of the Master. He was as *"one born out of due time"* (1 Cor. 15:8). Many things were related to him by those who had seen and heard Jesus. Picture his life and the various manifestations; there was always something about the Master that was told to him. Let me now read the passage from Philippians:

> *Finally, my brethren, rejoice in the Lord. For me to write the same things to you is not tedious, but for you it is safe. Beware of dogs, beware of evil workers, beware of the mutilation! For we are the circumcision, who worship God in the Spirit, rejoice in Christ Jesus, and have no confidence in the flesh, though I also might have confidence in the flesh. If anyone else thinks he may*

*have confidence in the flesh, I more so: circumcised the eighth
day, of the stock of Israel, of the tribe of Benjamin, a Hebrew of
the Hebrews; concerning the law, a Pharisee; concerning zeal,
persecuting the church; concerning the righteousness which is in
the law, blameless. But what things were gain to me, these I
have counted loss for Christ. Yet indeed I also count all things
loss for the excellence of the knowledge of Christ Jesus my Lord,
for whom I have suffered the loss of all things, and count them
as rubbish, that I may gain Christ and be found in Him, not
having my own righteousness, which is from the law, but that
which is through faith in Christ, the righteousness which is from
God by faith; that I may know Him and the power of His resurrection, and the fellowship of His sufferings, being conformed
to His death, if, by any means, I may attain to the resurrection
from the dead. Not that I have already attained, or am already
perfected; but I press on, that I may lay hold of that for which
Christ Jesus has also laid hold of me. Brethren, I do not count
myself to have apprehended; but one thing I do, forgetting those
things which are behind and reaching forward to those things
which are ahead, I press toward the goal for the prize of the
upward call of God in Christ Jesus.*   (Phil. 3:1–14)

Paul had reached a place where he desired all that the Master
has. As far as keeping the law, he was blameless, and he had a zeal
that went so far as to persecute the church. In the midst of it all, he
saw what the Master has. I want, by the grace of God, to help you.
Christ is the great Principle, not only the great Teacher.

There is something in the new birth of the divine character
that makes us long all the time to be like Him. It is not so much
an impression, but something in our lives, words, and actions that
makes people know that we have been with the Master and that we

have learned from Him. (See Acts 4:13.) Paul was there. He said, "'We are the circumcision, who worship God in the Spirit' (Phil. 3:3), and are righteous in Jesus Christ, 'and have no confidence in the flesh' (v. 3). I am perceiving by the Spirit of the living God that there is nothing good in me (Rom. 7:18); the Spirit moves me to see that in Him there is not only energizing power, but that in the act there is also divine character—the presence of the ideal character that kept Him calm and collected all the time. Within Jesus, there is also compassion, a knowledge of the needy. This is the place for me to reach; yes, I seek that, the character of the Lord." I want to emphasize this word.

GAINING CHRIST

Yet indeed I also count all things loss for the excellence of the knowledge of Christ Jesus my Lord, for whom I have suffered the loss of all things, and count them as rubbish, that I may gain Christ. (Phil. 3:8)

Paul was not seeking the knowledge of salvation; there was something that salvation brought as a spring into his soul. It brought all the life that was within the life, which had within itself divine resources, a longing after Him. Oh, that I might gain Him! All of us *must* reach the state of the crucifixion. Paul had heard about Jesus' suffering and crucifixion. He had heard how, before the judgment seat, Jesus did not utter a word, and how they struck Him with the rod, and how they gave Him vinegar when He was on the cross, and how, in the midst of the crucifixion, He had love for His enemies, saying, "*Father, forgive them, for they do not know what they do*" (Luke 23:34). To gain Him in persecution and in trial is to reply with a soft answer when suffering, and when reviled, not to revile in return (1 Pet. 2:23).

Is this the true picture within our hearts today? Is it the reality? Have we felt like this? Is there no help for us? We have been *"laid hold of"* (Phil. 3:12) by Christ so that we may be made perfect. Even though we have had a thousand failures, it does not matter, for God has laid hold of us. For the perfection, the ideal perfection, we must have nothing less than sonship, nothing less than purity. *"Be ye therefore perfect"* (Matt. 5:48 KJV).

The security of our position, the importance, is to gain Him. Though you fail, don't give in. The excellency of the character is before us; the divine purpose is working right through.

We are not here at this conference to be entertained. These are days of quickening, reviving, stirring, and moving. Oh, yes, the Master is before us in many revelations as we hear the speakers. The Lord opens the door so that we can have a new vision and enter into the divine character of the Lord.

THE RIGHTEOUSNESS THAT IS BY FAITH

That I may gain Christ and be found in Him, not having my own righteousness, which is from the law, but that which is through faith in Christ, the righteousness which is from God by faith. (Phil. 3:8–9)

I am continually confronted with this truth. God comes to me over and over again asking if I am prepared and willing. Oh, to have this faith, to be always realizing what is happening. God's plan and purpose for me is to know *"the righteousness which is...by faith,"* so *"that I may...be found in Him,"* undisturbed, no matter what is happening. There is something in *"the righteousness which is...by faith"* that helps you to graduate.

It lives. This rock is so real to be upon; and yet, from this position, you find that the Word of God lives and your own position fails. God says He will hold us with the righteousness that is by faith. This being *"found in Him"* is so remarkable; it is right for every emergency.

Look at the sixth chapter of John. The Lord Jesus said to Philip, when He saw the multitudes coming to hear Him, *"Where shall we buy bread, that these may eat?"* (v. 5). What a picture this is of the Master, who was at rest in the knowledge of how they would be provided for. Jesus had compassion on the multitudes, just as He did in the account of the feeding of the four thousand, when He said to His disciples,

> *I have compassion on the multitude, because they have now continued with Me three days and have nothing to eat. And I do not want to send them away hungry, lest they faint on the way.*
> (Matt. 15:32)

Jesus was testing Philip, *"for He Himself knew what He would do"* (John 6:6). That is the wonderful thing in Him.

Can we reach the place where we are in the Master's will, where we can absolutely see that God will plan for us? I like the righteousness that is by faith.

Are you at your wits' end, or in a place of trial? Do you think you have committed the unpardonable sin? Brothers and sisters, there is a place where God puts you in a position where you are in Him, no matter how severe the storm or strain may be.

Philip answered Jesus, *"Two hundred denarii worth of bread is not sufficient for them, that every one of them may have a little"* (John 6:7). Then Andrew said, *"There is a lad here who has five barley loaves and two small fish*" (v. 9). This was a striking evidence of foresight, and quite easy for the Master.

Some have said that it was quite easy for Jesus to feed the multitudes with these loaves because the loaves were so big. However, they do not mention the fact that the boy had carried them.

The Master handled the loaves, and when the Master handles us, He can enlarge us, if we are ready. He has a wonderful way of enlarging things. "*He Himself knew what He would do*" (John 6:6). And this is what the apostle Paul was referring to in Philippians 3. He was saying, "If I can only get to that place, if I can only reach the principle of the righteousness of this Christ, the place where nothing is too big, then I could meet the need of all." God not only wants us to gain Christ and His principles, but He also wants us to handle something today. Jesus was always in the restful place, in God. Praise God.

My soul is warm right now. It is the principle of the Master, where nothing is too much for me to do if I can only reach the state where Christ is living in me. He moves in this great scene; He has another plan here; the Lord wants to bring us a little further.

THE POWER OF HIS RESURRECTION

"*That I may know Him and the power of His resurrection*" (Phil. 3:10). There is something prior to the great Resurrection, and these are principles. We may know the power of His resurrection only with a divine revelation of the principles, in order to make us see that while Jesus was on the earth, He had the power of the Resurrection.

It is lovely for me to hear how God is establishing the truth I spoke in the gifts. Jesus said, "*Greater works than these* [you] *will do*"

(John 14:12), and He was raising people from the dead. Lord, give us grace not to stumble.

May He bring us to the place where we count all things loss so that we may gain Him (Phil. 3:8). There is to be a new man made within the man, in order to manifest the divine plan for the people in our day. It is glorious to read of the prophets Isaiah and Ezekiel, and also of Enoch and Lot, but this is our day. God's plan for us is the outpouring of the Holy Spirit, and there is within this great plan a rising of our minds, in order that we may be associated with this great principle of faith.

When Dorcas died, they sent for Peter; he came, and the widows wept as they showed him the things she had made for them. This woman had lived in benevolence, and gave her life for the people. The eagerness and the longings of the people brought Peter to a place where he sat by the corpse. What was it that moved him? It was the longings of the cry of the people. Her ministry to them had been the ministry of Christ.

These reports of her Christlike spirit came alive to Peter; they drew and laid hold of him, and he sat down by this corpse. Realizing the need of a presence, Peter prayed, and then he said, "Dorcas." She opened her eyes and was restored to life. (See Acts 9:36–42.) It was the principle. We must come to a place of helplessness in every way so that Christ can do the work.

Let us look at two other examples of people who were resurrected by the power of Jesus. In Mark 5, we read how Jesus, taking Peter, James, and John with Him, raised a twelve-year-old girl from the dead. (See Mark 5:35–43.) I imagine Jesus saying, "Look, Peter, James, and John, I will show you; stand to one side." He took the girl by the hand and said, *"Little girl, I say to you, arise"* (v. 41).

In another instance, Jesus raised from the dead the only son of a widow from Nain. Many of Jesus' disciples were with Him, along with a large crowd. Jesus said, on another occasion, *"I am the resurrection and the life"* (John 11:25). But the presentation before them was death. The people had just brought outside the gates of Nain a young man who was dead. Did Jesus say to His disciples, "I will show you *how* to do it?" Oh, no, that is not the way of the Master. It is always His power. Jesus had compassion on the widow, and His compassion for the widow was greater than death. (See Luke 7:11–15.) May I *"be found in Him, not having my own righteousness"* (Phil. 3:9). The truth that is hidden in me is greater than me, manifesting the power of God. It is not in human nature but in the power of God.

THE FELLOWSHIP OF HIS SUFFERINGS

"That I may know Him...and the fellowship of His sufferings" (Phil. 3:10). Does God want me to suffer for another? One Man has suffered. There is something about *"the fellowship of His sufferings."* Can we reach the agony of the depressed and broken? This fellowship is to be reached in only one way, and that is to bear with them. When the woman who was a sinner poured oil on Jesus' feet at the home of the Pharisee, the Pharisee said to himself, "If He knew *'what manner of woman this is '"* (Luke 7:39). We know that they all knew her, and that she was a woman of the city, but nobody knew her as well as Jesus did; that is the fellowship of suffering. She had seen the Master, and she knelt at the feet of Jesus, anointing His feet with oil. She got what she wanted; her sins were forgiven. (See Luke 7:36–50.) And she was among those in the Upper Room who spoke with tongues.

BEING CONFORMED TO HIS DEATH

"Being conformed to His death" (Phil. 3:10). Is it the death of His cross? No, but deathlikeness. What would happen if the trumpet blew for you to be a king? That night in the Garden of Gethsemane, Jesus went to pray, and He said, *"Not My will, but Yours, be done"* (Luke 22:42), even though He was a King.

There was a death there: it was the very clamor of human justice. And God can cause His death to save us from where the flesh rises to be something, to keep us where we can be for God. He has a perfect way of doing it.

BEING LAID HOLD OF BY GOD

God can grant you the desires of your heart, because He has *"laid hold of* [you]" (Phil. 3:12). You are in this meeting so that you may see that He has laid hold of you, so that you may be laid hold of by Him. Whatever is in your hearts right now, God is greater than your hearts (1 John 3:20), greater than all things. Let us rise and give ourselves to God.

15

THE GIVEN GLORY

Then the mother of Zebedee's sons came to Him with her sons, kneeling down and asking something from Him. And He said to her, "What do you wish?" She said to Him, "Grant that these two sons of mine may sit, one on Your right hand and the other on the left, in Your kingdom." But Jesus answered and said, "You do not know what you ask. Are you able to drink the cup that I am about to drink, and be baptized with the baptism that I am baptized with?" They said to Him, "We are able." So He said to them, "You will indeed drink My cup, and be baptized with the baptism that I am baptized with; but to sit on My right hand and on My left is not Mine to give, but it is for those for whom it is prepared by My Father."
—Matthew 20:20–23

We have here in this Scripture passage a wonderful subject. All God's Word is life-giving; it is life and light. If we are poor, it is because we do not know the Word of God. God's Word is full of riches, ever opening to us fresh avenues of divine life. *"It is the Spirit who gives life"* (John 6:63). Jesus said, *"The words that I speak to you are spirit, and they are life"* (v. 63). It has a mighty changing power, effectively working in us. We do not need to remain in the same place two days. It is the Word of God, and He *"gives us richly all things to enjoy"* (1 Tim. 6:17).

This Book is the copy of the Word—the original is in the glory. *"In the beginning was the Word, and the Word was with God, and the Word was God"* (John 1:1). You will find that the moment you reach the glory, you will have the principle of the Word. The Author is there—the Author of Faith is there. He is our life, and He fills us with illumination. The Holy Spirit unveils the Christ to us.

A brother came to see me to ask about the Holy Spirit. He was so anxious that his ministry should be a success. I pointed out to him the words of Jesus to His disciples, "The Holy Spirit is *'with you and will be in you'* (John 14:17)." I said to him, "You see the sun this morning—how it pours into the room from the outside? But if the light were inside, how the light would shine forth outside, illuminating the dark places!"

When we receive the baptism in the Holy Spirit, we receive a new ministry with divine power and glory. *"The kingdom of God is not eating and drinking, but righteousness and peace and joy in the Holy Spirit"* (Rom. 14:17). The Holy Spirit reveals the Christ who reigns in every believer when Jesus is coronated, and Jesus is coronated when you receive the Holy Spirit. *"Did you receive the Holy Spirit when you believed?"* (Acts 19:2). Jesus is King over your desires—no man can call Jesus Lord but by the Holy Spirit (1 Cor. 12:3). When the Holy Spirit comes in, Jesus is Lord. Then His Word floods our souls, the tide flows out to the needy, and the vision increases. Then I am hungrier than ever—nothing satisfies me but God.

I like the word that Jesus spoke to the mother of James and John, "*What do you wish?*" (Matt. 20:21). She answered, "*Grant that these two sons of mine may sit, one on Your right hand and the other on the left, in Your kingdom*" (v. 21). I am sure that James and John had this desire, and you can have the same desire. Jesus is the mighty worker of desire. He moves people to desire. He said, "*You do not know what you ask*" (v. 22). Did they know? No! Did Mary know how she would become the mother of the Savior? No! But she said, "*Let it be to me according to your word*" (Luke 1:38). James and John said, "*We are able*" (Matt. 20:22). Would they have said it if they had known? On another occasion, the people asked Jesus, "*What shall we do, that we may work the works of God?*" (John 6:28). Jesus said, "*Believe in Him whom He sent*" (v. 29).

I believe it is more than *saying* it. It is the life of God in the nature that stretches out to believe and to receive. We can be thus drawn into the love of the Spirit, "*the law of the Spirit of life*" making us "*free from the law of sin and death*" (Rom. 8:2); and you know you are in what will never pass away.

Jesus said, "*I came to send fire on the earth.... Father will be divided against son and son against father*" (Luke 12:49, 53), and "*A man's enemies will be those of his own household*" (Matt. 10:36). I remember that, twenty-two years ago, when I received the baptism of the Holy Spirit according to Acts 2:4, I sent home a wire (the post office was opposite my house) that I had received the baptism of the Holy Spirit and was speaking in other tongues. The news ran like wildfire— everybody seemed to know. When I arrived home, my wife said to me, "So you have received the baptism of the Holy Spirit and are speaking in tongues? I want you to know I am baptized as much as you." Right in my house, the war began. She said, "For twenty years, I have been the preacher." Now, before that time, I could not preach; I had tried many times. Preachers are God-made men—Jesus was *"moved with compassion."* (See, for example, Matthew 9:36.) My wife said, "Next Sunday, you go on the platform by yourself, and I'll see if there is anything in this." I was under great pressure as to what I was to speak about, and as I went onto the platform, Jesus said to me, *"The Spirit of the LORD is upon* [you]" (Luke 4:18). I don't know what I said, but my wife—she got up and she sat down, she got up and she sat down. She said, "That is not my husband." No man can be filled with the Holy Spirit and be the same man. He is turned into another man.

THE CUPS

Yes, in Matthew 20, Jesus spoke of the "cups"—the cup of blessing and the cup of suffering. They go together. It is always the *"hundredfold"* blessings, but *"with persecutions"* (Mark 10:30)—but it is going all the way. The cross is not greater than His grace. The cloud cannot hide His blessed face. I am satisfied to know that, with Jesus, here below I can conquer every foe. Did John know what it meant to *"drink the cup"* (Matt. 20:22)? No! Thank God, there is something we cannot resist, and that is saying, "Lord, give me the baptism of the Holy Spirit"—this luxury, this summit of perfection, makes your whole being cry out for the living God, and you say, "Yes, Lord!"

Never mind anything that it costs you! I saw one man who was in a waiting meeting seeking the baptism of the Holy Spirit; he was about to leave. I said, "Brother, why are you leaving?" "Oh," he said, "I must go home—I have something to do. I wrote a letter to my wife's brother, and I must tell him I am sorry." He told his wife what he was doing. She said, "You fool." But the baptism of the Holy Spirit means a clean heart. The next night, there he was at the meeting again. "Oh," he said, "it is too much this time." I said, "Brother, obey God at any cost. It does not matter how bitter the cup; God will give you grace." He was a farmer, and he was accustomed to sending a check regularly for corn, but one time he missed, and he had put off paying his account. When he paid the account, the blessing of God came upon his life. Oh, yes, we must be eligible for this wonderful place in the glory. We must drink the cup, but it will mean the baptism, and the baptism of the Holy Spirit means the fullness of the divine anointing.

The Scripture says, *"Jesus returned in the power of the Spirit to Galilee"* (Luke 4:14). He went to the synagogue in Nazareth on the Sabbath Day and read,

> *The Spirit of the LORD is upon Me, because He has anointed Me to preach the gospel to the poor; He has sent Me to heal the brokenhearted, to proclaim liberty to the captives and recovery of sight to the blind, to set at liberty those who are oppressed; to proclaim the acceptable year of the LORD.* (Luke 4:18–19)

Then He said, *"Today this Scripture is fulfilled in your hearing"* (v. 21). There are days when the Spirit is mighty upon us, as He is this day.

Once, when I was in a ship going from Alexandria to Venice, and again the other day at Liverpool, seeing the crowd, some thousand people, my heart was moved with compassion. When I was on the ship, I began to speak. Everyone was as still as death—captain, crew, and passengers—as they listened to the message God gave me for them. There are times when you know the Spirit of God is mighty upon you, and you act, even though, to the onlooker, it may seem out of place. But you have got your orders, and you act, and the Holy Spirit bears witness to it (Acts 14:3; Heb. 2:4).

THE FIRE

Another time, in Jerusalem, at the place of wailing, the Spirit of the Lord moved me. I saw young men, many of them in the prime of manhood, beating their breasts, weeping bitterly, and saying, "Lord, how long? Lord, how long?" I preached Jesus to them. The next day, ten of them came to see me, and with them was a rabbi. They said, "Where did the fire come from? When you preached, we felt the fire. We have no fire in our synagogues." Oh, beloved, the baptism of the Holy Spirit is a baptism of fire. *"He will baptize you with the Holy Spirit and fire"* (Matt. 3:11). So I began to talk with them about God's promises of a Messiah, and how He was crucified at Calvary. God wants us so filled with the Holy Spirit that people feel the power—feel the fire.

Let me tell you more about my experience on the ship. I got on the ship at Alexandria. I wanted to preach, but I could not. I did not know the language, and I had no interpreter. I read Acts 1:1: *"Jesus began both to do and teach."* To do and then to teach. I wanted *"to do,"* but how? I was ready, but I had no opportunity. A man cannot make the opportunity. He has to be ready. It is God who makes the opportunity, and right where I stood, a man fell down on the deck. His wife cried out, "My husband is dead!" Someone ran for the doctor, but before he arrived, I began to do. I said, "In the name of Jesus," and the man revived. There was much excitement and pointing at me; everyone wanted to know what had happened. I could not speak to them, but I found five people who could interpret for me. And everyone on the ship heard the old story of Jesus and His love.

Don't forget, we have to begin to do, then to teach. Nine years ago, I went to Sweden. The people did not know me, but God led me there. We are as truly sent by God as ever the apostles were. I had a rough journey, and I thought that, after landing, I would have some hours in the train, but a meeting was ready for me. As I entered the building, a man fell across the doorway in a fit. I rebuked the devil in Jesus' name, and the man got up. I said, "Give your testimony." He obeyed and said that it was as if something had snapped from top to bottom in his body, and he was free. This incident was the key to many open doors of opportunity. Seven years later, I was again at that place. I asked if anyone remembered the incident. A man rose in the gallery and said, "It was me, and I have been free since."

Jesus began to do. There is no one who loves me like Jesus. There is no one who can heal me like Him. He is acquainted with my weaknesses. He knows all my sorrows. There is no one who can heal me like Him. Oh, yes, it's a real baptism of fire and a real baptism of suffering. The suffering keeps you in balance. Jesus did the most astounding things, making the people marvel. As He is, we have to be. (See 1 John 4:17.) He fed five thousand. (See, for example, Matthew 14:13–21.) He healed the man born blind (John 9:1–7). Where Jesus was, the crowds came, and the children came; He could not be hidden; the crowds followed Him.

Blind Bartimaeus heard the noise of the crowds. He asked, "Who is it? Who is it?" "It's Jesus!" they told him. He cried, "Jesus! Jesus! *Jesus, Son of David, have mercy on me!'* (Mark 10:47)." The people said, "Be quiet." (See verse 48.) But presently, their words changed to, *"Be of good cheer. Rise, He is calling you"* (v. 49). As Bartimaeus cried out, *"Jesus stood still and commanded him to be called"* (v. 49). Jesus stopped for Bartimaeus, and He'll stop for you. Jesus asked Bartimaeus, *"What do you want Me to do for you?"* (v. 51). What is your request? He is here. He asks you the question, *"What do you want Me to do for you?"* Bartimaeus answered, *"Rabboni, that I may receive my sight"* (v. 51). Jesus healed him, saying, *"Your faith has made you well"* (v. 52). And Jesus is here right now.

Yes, it is a cup of blessing and a cup of suffering, and the place prepared in the glory. May we yield to God so that the Holy Spirit can prepare us for the place—and the glory—so that we may begin to do and to teach until the day when we are taken up, having the same testing as He had. Then we can say, as He did, *"It is finished!"* (John 19:30). We are to minister the cup of blessing, which also means for us the cup of suffering.

16

IMMERSED IN THE HOLY SPIRIT

The baptism of the Holy Spirit is a great beginning. I think the best word we can say is, *"Lord, what do You want me to do?"* (Acts 9:6). The greatest difficulty with us today is to be held in the place where it will be God only. It is so easy to get our own minds to work. The working of the Holy Spirit is so different. I believe there is a mind of Christ (1 Cor. 2:16), and we may be so immersed in the Spirit that we are asking all day, *"What do You want me to do?"*

This has been a day in the Holy Spirit. The last three months have been the greatest days of my life. I used to think that if I could see certain things happen, I would be satisfied; but I have seen greater things than I ever expected to see, and I am hungrier to see greater things still. The great thing about conferences is that we may get so immersed in God that we may see signs and wonders in the name of the Lord Jesus. This immersion in God is a place where death to self has taken place, and "we" are no longer, for God has taken us. (See Hebrews 11:5.) If God has taken hold of us, we will be changed by

His power and might. You can depend on it, the Ethiopian will be changed. (See Jeremiah 13:23.) I find that God has a plan to turn *"the world upside down"* (Acts 17:6), when we have died to self.

When I have been at my wits' end and have seen God open the door, I have felt as if I would never doubt God again. Then I have been taken to another place that was worse still. There is no place for us, and yet there is a place where God is, where the Holy Spirit is showing forth and displaying His graces, a place where we will never come out, where we are always immersed in the Spirit, the glory of God being seen upon us. It is wonderful! There is a power behind the scenes that moves things. God can work in such a marvelous way.

I believe we have yet to learn what it would be like with a Pentecostal church in England that truly understood the work of intercession. I believe God the Holy Spirit wants to teach us that it is not only the people on the platform who can move things by prayer, but that you people—the Lord can also move things through you. We have to learn the power of the breath of the Holy Spirit. If I am filled with the Holy Spirit, He will formulate the word that will come into my heart. The sound of my voice is made only by the breath that goes through it.

When I was in a little room at Bern, Switzerland, waiting for my passport, I found a lot of people, but I couldn't speak to them. So I got hold of three men and pulled them to me. They stared, but I got them on their knees. Then we prayed, and the revival began. I couldn't talk to them, but I could show them the way to talk to Someone else.

God will move upon the people to make them see the glory of God just as it was when Jesus walked in this world; and I believe the Holy Spirit will do special wonders and miracles in these last days.

I was taken to see a young woman who was very ill. The young man who showed me the way said, "I am afraid we will not be able to do much here because of her mother, and the doctors are coming." I said, "This is what God has brought me here for," and when I prayed, the young woman was instantly healed by the power of God. God the Holy Spirit says in our hearts today that it is only He who can do it. After the young woman's healing, a crowd gathered, and I ministered to the sick among them for two hours.

The secret for the future is living and moving in the power of the Holy Spirit. One thing I rejoice in is that there does not need to be an hour or a moment when I do not know that the Holy Spirit is upon me. Oh, this glorious life in God is beyond expression; it is God manifest in the flesh. Oh, this glorious anointing of the Holy Spirit—that we move by the Spirit. He should be our continual life. The Holy Spirit has the latest thoughts of anything that God wants to give. Glory to God for the Holy Spirit! We must see to it that we live in the place where we say, *"What do You want me to do?"* (Acts 9:6), and that we are in the place where He can work in us *"to will and to do for His good pleasure"* (Phil. 2:13).

17

TRANSFORMED

God wants us to place our lives on the altar for service. *We can really be there on the altar*—not just "hope" to be there. In Romans 12, Paul had reached a reserved place, a separated place. He was now in the place where the Holy Spirit can speak.

What does it mean to be in this place? *"Those who sow in tears shall reap in joy"* (Ps. 126:5). *"The LORD has set apart for Himself him who is godly"* (Ps. 4:3). His enemies will be at peace with him (Prov. 16:7), and God will send him prosperity in hard times.

"I beseech you…"—with all who see this truth—*"that you present your bodies a living sacrifice"* (Rom. 12:1). Here is the mercy of God, the unfathomable, desirable will of God (see verse 2): the body presented as a living sacrifice. It's a present—a living sacrifice, not a worn-out life. The body, soul, and spirit are to be presented blameless at the coming of the Lord (1 Thess. 5:23). The present life is given—with no choice but God's will—thus, on the altar. Oh, Lord, not mine but Yours now! Lord, use it for Your glory. I am through

with resisting your will and with saying "I won't"—all is Yours! A living body, placed at God's disposal. A holy body, with the best mind, and without a thought outside *"Holiness to the Lord"* (Zech. 14:20).

God only asks for what you can give! *"Do not be conformed to this world"* (Rom. 12:2). Do not be conformed—that is, moved by it. That is not to say you are to be a hermit or unconcerned about the world, but *"transformed"* (v. 2). Every hour, you are to be more purely transformed—so that you may prove what God's will is for you (v. 2). It's a holy, acceptable will. Then you will have no sourness or irritability, or that thing about you that nobody wants. It's an acceptable will. If you give, you give cheerfully; if you love, you love warmly; if you shake hands, people know you mean it. (See vv. 6–11.) Your whole life becomes beautiful—clinging to God. (See verse 9.) *"Rejoicing in hope,"* even in *"tribulation,"* meeting it with prayer (v. 12), giving a blessing without a curse (v. 14). This kind of life is received by men, and is acceptable in the sight of God. Moreover, at the Closing-up Day, it has a sure reward.

Let us pray and commit our whole way to God, not being conformed, but transformed, proving God's good and acceptable and perfect will. Amen.

18

POWER

God intends us to be in this way where Jesus and all His disciples went. He has left this place open: *"Greater works than these [you] will do, because I go to My Father"* (John 14:12). Jesus left nothing less than this: a power that was for us and to which more was to be added if we believe. Acts 1 speaks of this power:

> *The former account I made, O Theophilus, of all that Jesus began both to do and teach, until the day in which He was taken up, after He through the Holy Spirit had given commandments to the apostles whom He had chosen, to whom He also presented Himself alive after His suffering by many infallible proofs, being seen by them during forty days and speaking of the things pertaining to the kingdom of God. And being assembled together with them, He commanded them not to depart from Jerusalem, but to wait for the Promise of the Father, "which," He said, "you have heard from Me; for John truly baptized with water, but you shall be baptized with the Holy Spirit not many days*

from now." Therefore, when they had come together, they asked Him, saying, "Lord, will You at this time restore the kingdom to Israel?" And He said to them, "It is not for you to know times or seasons which the Father has put in His own authority. But you shall receive power when the Holy Spirit has come upon you; and you shall be witnesses to Me in Jerusalem, and in all Judea and Samaria, and to the end of the earth."   (Acts 1:1–8)

We have recently experienced seven years of earthly power, and we are feeling the effects of it today—how it has broken hearts, homes, and, in fact, the whole world, and has filled it with such distressing effects and made it an awful place, so that we never want it again.

This power from Jesus is so very different: it restores the fallen, it heals the brokenhearted, it lifts, it lives, it brings life into existence in your own hearts. All the time, there is something that is around you, something that you know is lasting and will be forever, until the Lord receives us unto Himself.

May God help me to speak to you. I did not come only to speak but also to stir us up to our privilege, to make people feel they are responsible for the state of things around them.

POWER AND PROGRESS

It thrills my soul and makes me think that I must step into line where God has called me. Sometimes I speak like this. Some of you know what a tragedy is—you have heard of such things—and some of you know what a calamity is. I speak to every baptized soul here: If you have not made any progress, you are a backslider in the sight of God because of the privilege of the revelation of the Spirit within you, the privilege and more power of entering into more light.

It is a wonderful thing to get into touch with the living God. It is a glorious thing, a blessed condescension of God, to fill us with the Holy Spirit. But we have a responsibility after that so that we remain filled with the Spirit of God, so that Jesus is so pleased with His child that He fills His child with the Holy Spirit, so that the child may now have the full revelation of Himself. The Holy Spirit will not speak of Himself, but He will take of the truth of Jesus Christ and reveal it to us (John 16:13–15). As Jesus is, we have to be (1 John 4:17), and just as righteous as He is, we have to be. We are truly the offspring of God, moving with divine impulse, and God is testing us so that we can see that we must step into line and that the truth is still the same.

"You shall receive power" (Acts 1:8). Beloved, this is so real after we *"receive power"*: His life for us is the life of the Son of God living within us, with divine characteristics that make the whole body a flame of fire. I am clearly coming to understand this in my ministry. God has given me a gracious ministry, and I thank Him for it. God has given me a ministry that I prize because it helps me to stir people, especially leaders. I am here to stir you; I could not think that God would have me leave you as I found you. I could not speak if I thought I was entrusted to speak for half an hour and leave you as I found you! So my desire is that this half hour will be so full of divine purpose that everyone will come into line with the plan of God.

POWER AND PURITY

I am as convinced as anything that if I wait further to receive the Holy Spirit, I have mistaken the situation. Along these lines, I very much want to say things to prove the situation. Too much is being said along the lines of, "If I can only *feel* the power." Our young brother said distinctly that the Holy Spirit came to abide.

(See 1 John 2:27.) What are we waiting for? What is God waiting for? For you to get into the place. What do I mean? I mean this: Jesus was a perfect activity, a life in activity. The Scripture declares it. It is as clear as possible that He began to do and then to teach (Acts 1:1) in a realm of divine appointment where He was able to make the act conform.

So I am truly speaking from the Word of God. If we have received the power, the power is there. I am not going to say that there does not have to be an unbroken fellowship with God. He never separates power from holiness; the pure in heart will see God (Matt. 5:8). But I believe that if the Holy Spirit has come to reveal Jesus to us, you cannot lack this power, because he who believes that Jesus is the Christ overcomes the world (1 John 5:5).

He is the purifier; He is the abiding presence, the one great source of righteousness. *"In* [Jesus] *dwells all the fullness of the Godhead bodily"* (Col. 2:9). There is the situation.

> Christ liveth in me!
> Christ liveth in me!
> Oh, what a salvation this,
> That Christ liveth in me!

And you know that after the Spirit gave the revelation of the purity of Christ by the Word of the Lord, He made you see things as you had never seen them before.

THE BREATH OF THE SPIRIT

I would like to speak for a few moments on the breath of the Spirit because I see that the Holy Spirit came as a breath, or as the moving of a mighty wind (Acts 2:2). I see so much divine appointment in this for humanity, in this great thought: the Holy Spirit fills the life by the breath. This prophetic position is wonderful. Whom did you hear speak? You say, "I heard Mr. Wigglesworth and Mr. Carter." Yes, that is what we say, but behind it all, you will find that when the speaker is under the control of the Holy Spirit, language is breath, the breath of the Spirit.

When you are filled with the breath of the Spirit, the breath of God, the holy fire, and the Word, it is Christ within you.

Life is given. *"He who hears My word and believes in Him who sent Me has everlasting life"* (John 5:24). We need the Spirit so that we may be filled with prophetic power in order to bring forth life for the needs of the people. This is life; I am perceiving that I must be in this order. Let me give you one or two additional points.

POWER IN ACTION

God wants everybody, without exception, to begin on the Word of God. Acting upon the Word will bring about the most surprising things you have ever experienced. As you stand on the Word, it will be an amazing thing.

This power from God is for every believer. After you have received the power of the Holy Spirit (Acts 1:8), you are in the place where this is possible. I am not saying this glibly; my thoughts are too serious for that. After tonight, I can no longer be what I was today, and tomorrow is mightier than today. This is the reason the tide is changing with God; this is the reality.

It is no little thing to be baptized with the Spirit; it is *"the Promise of the Father"* (v. 4). Jesus must be there, and the Holy Spirit also, bringing us to the place where we can be baptized. Are you going to treat it as a great thing? What do you really believe it is? I believe that when the Holy Spirit comes, He comes to crown the King. And from that day, the King gets His rightful place, and we don't have to claim anything; He becomes King of all situations.

I only say this to help you. It is a need that I am speaking about. I cannot get away from this fact because, where I look, I see growth. I see you people; I see the growth. I have been away from England for three years, and I see changes; yet even though we see that there is growth, life, and blessing, there is much more ground to be possessed, and we will have to dare before God can work.

God has given me an open door. Nothing moves me but this: that I see men and women coming into line with this reality. I want the people of Pentecost to rise as the heart of one man. God has us for a purpose in these last days, and He helps me in the meetings.

A MAN HEALED OF CANCER AFTER TWELVE YEARS

At a certain meeting, I said, "There is a man in this meeting who is suffering. Should I preach before I help this man, or would you like to see this person free before I commence?" This man was a stranger and did not know who I was speaking about. There he was, with cancer on his face and full of pain, and I asked, "Is it right for me to preach, or should I heal this man?" I saw what was the right thing, and I went down off the platform and placed my hand on him in the name of Jesus.

What happened next was because of what the Word said. That man knew nothing of healing, but in a moment, he was able to stand up, and he said, "I have been in pain for twelve years. Something has happened to me." That night, he gave himself to God, and he testified night after night that he was completely cured. What happened? God ministered through my daring to believe His Word.

There are cases all around you, and what a story you would have to tell next year if only you would take a stand on the Word of God from now on.

A HUSBAND HEALED OF MANY AILMENTS AFTER FORTY YEARS

A woman brought her husband to me and said, "I want you to help my husband." I said, "Well, I will." She said, "He has too many ailments to tell you of." I said to those present at the meeting, "There is a man here who is so full of pains and weakness that I am going to pray for him on the authority of God's Word, and tomorrow night I am going to ask him to come back and tell you what God has done for him." Then I placed my hand on him in the name of Jesus.

The next night, this man came walking straight, and he said, "Will you let me speak to these people tonight? For forty years, I have had ulcers and running sores, and today is the first day that my clothes have been dry, and now I am a new man." Brothers and sisters, this is declared in the Word, and wonderful things happen.

A SUFFERING BOY HEALED

I had been speaking about divine healing. Six seats from the rear was a man with a boy, and he lifted him up when I had finished. The boy was held together with irons, and his head, loins, and shoulders were bandaged. The father handed him over to me. He put the irons down with the boy standing in them.

I have never known what there is in the laying on of hands, but let me give you a description of what happened. This boy was about nine years of age. After I had laid hands on him in the name of Jesus, there was perfect silence, when suddenly this boy cried out, "Dad, it is going all over me," and I said, "Take the irons off." Perhaps you might say that this is our power. No, it is His power; no, it is the

Father you have received. Do we dare to be still and to be quiet? The stones would cry out if we did. (See Luke 19:37–40.)

Sometimes I go in for what they call "wholesale healings." My son and daughter are here, and they can declare that they have seen one hundred people healed without the touch of a hand. I believe there are to be wholesale baptisms of the Holy Spirit.

"ASK, AND I WILL GIVE YOU EVERY SOUL"

One day, God told me something at a place called Stavanger in Norway. I said to my interpreter, "We are both very tired. We will rest today until 4:00 P.M." I can never forget the sight when we returned from being out. This story has just occurred to me. May God cause you to hear this. There is a hearing of faith, a much higher faith. May the Lord cause us to hear this.

We had been out for a short time, and I will never forget the sight as we came back into the street. The street was filled with all kinds of wheelchairs. We went along up to the house, and the house was filled with people, and the woman there said, "What can we do? The house is filled; what are we to do?" So I pulled off my coat and I got down to business. My brothers and sisters, you ought to have been there; the power of God came like a cloud, and people were healed on every side.

God healed all the people. This is what I have to tell you. We had sat down for a little refresher before the meeting, and the telephone rang. The pastor went to the telephone, and those on the other end of the line said, "What can we do? The great town hall is packed. Come down as soon as you can." This is what I mean by the hearing of faith; I declare that the place was so packed that the people could not have fallen down if they had wanted to. I never saw a place so packed. I began to preach, and when I was preaching, the voice came from the Lord, "Ask, and I will give you every soul." The voice came again, "Ask, and I will give you every soul." I dared to ask, "Give me every soul," and a breath came like the rushing of a mighty wind, and it shook everyone and fell on everyone. I have never seen anything like it.

I am hoping to see this in London. Is there anything too hard for God (Gen. 18:14)? Can God not begin to do these things? Will we let Him?

I know it might be a difficult thing. Is it not possible to have a consecration today? Who will begin today? Who will begin to act in the power of the Holy Spirit?

Welcome to Our House!

We Have a Special Gift for You ...

It is our privilege and pleasure to share in your love of Christian classics by publishing books that enrich your life and encourage your faith.

To show our appreciation, we invite you to sign up to receive a specially selected **Reader Appreciation Gift**, with our compliments. Just go to the Web address at the bottom of this page.

God bless you as you seek a deeper walk with Him!

WE HAVE A GIFT FOR YOU

whpub.me/classicthx

WHITAKER
HOUSE